Philosophy

Bloomsbury Introductions to World Philosophies

Series Editor
Monika Kirloskar-Steinbach

Assistant Series Editor
Leah Kalmanson

Regional Editors
Nader El-Bizri, James Madaio, Sarah A. Mattice, Takeshi Morisato, Pascah
Mungwini, Omar Rivera and Georgina Stewart

Bloomsbury Introductions to World Philosophies delivers primers reflecting
exciting new developments in the trajectory of world philosophies. Instead
of privileging a single philosophical approach as the basis of comparison,
the series provides a platform for diverse philosophical perspectives to
accommodate the different dimensions of cross-cultural philosophizing.
While introducing thinkers, texts and themes emanating from different world
philosophies, each book, in an imaginative and path-breaking way, makes
clear how it departs from a conventional treatment of the subject matter.

Forthcoming Titles in the Series

Daya Krishna and Twentieth-Century Indian Philosophy, by Daniel Raveh
Li Zehou and Twentieth-Century Chinese Philosophy, by Andrew Lambert
Philosophy of Science and the Kyoto School, by Dean Anthony Brink
The Philosophy of the Brahma-sutra, by Aleksandar Uskokov
A Practical Guide to World Philosophies, by Monika Kirloskar-Steinbach and
Leah Kalmanson
Samkhya and Classical Indian Philosophy, by Marzenna Jakubczak
Tanabe Hajime and the Kyoto School, by Takeshi Morisato

Māori Philosophy

Indigenous Thinking from Aotearoa

Georgina Tuari Stewart

BLOOMSBURY ACADEMIC
LONDON • NEW YORK • OXFORD • NEW DELHI • SYDNEY

BLOOMSBURY ACADEMIC
Bloomsbury Publishing Plc
50 Bedford Square, London, WC1B 3DP, UK
1385 Broadway, New York, NY 10018, USA
29 Earlsfort Terrace, Dublin 2, Ireland

BLOOMSBURY, BLOOMSBURY ACADEMIC and the Diana logo are trademarks of
Bloomsbury Publishing Plc

First published in Great Britain 2021
Reprinted 2021 (eight times), 2022 (twice), 2023, 2024

Series design by Louise Dugdale
Cover image © oxygen / Getty Images

A catalogue record for this book is available from the British Library.

Library of Congress Cataloging-in-Publication Data
Names: Stewart, Georgina Tuari, author.
Title: Maori philosophy: indigenous thinking from Aotearoa / Georgina Tuari Stewart.
Description: London; New York: Bloomsbury Academic, 2020. | Series: Bloomsbury introductions
to world philosophies | Includes bibliographical references and index. | Summary: "This book is
a concise introduction to Maori philosophy, covering the symbolic systems and worldviews of
the indigenous people of Aotearoa, New Zealand. This book addresses core philosophical issues
including Maori notions of the self, the world, epistemology, the form in which Maori philosophy
is conveyed, and whether or not Maori philosophy has a teleological agenda. The book introduces
key texts, thinkers and themes and includes pedagogical features including: - A Maori-to-English
glossary; - Accessible English translations of primary source material; - Teaching notes, and
reflections on how the studied material engages with contemporary debates - End-of-chapter
discussion questions that can be used in teaching - Comprehensive bibliographies and guided
suggestions for further reading. Maori Philosophy is an ideal text for students studying World
Philosophies, or anyone who wishes to use indigenous philosophies or methodologies in their own
research and scholarship"– Provided by publisher.
Identifiers: LCCN 2020019575 (print) | LCCN 2020019576 (ebook) |
ISBN 9781350101654 (pb) | ISBN 9781350101661 (hb) | ISBN 9781350101685 (ebook) |
ISBN 9781350101678 (ePDF)
Subjects: LCSH: Philosophy, Maori. Classification: LCC B5712 .S84 2020 (print) |
LCC B5712 (ebook) | DDC 199/.9308999442–dc23
LC record available at https://lccn.loc.gov/2020019575
LC ebook record available at https://lccn.loc.gov/2020019576

ISBN: HB: 978-1-3501-0166-1
PB: 978-1-3501-0165-4
ePDF: 978-1-3501-0167-8
eBook: 978-1-3501-0168-5

Series: Bloomsbury Introductions to World Philosophies

Typeset by Deanta Global Publishing Services, Chennai, India
Printed and bound in Great Britain

To find out more about our authors and books visit www.bloomsbury.com and sign up for our
newsletters.

Contents

Figures

Series editor's preface

The introductions we include in the World Philosophies series take a single thinker, theme or text and provide a close reading of them. What defines the series is that these are likely to be people or traditions that you have not yet encountered in your study of philosophy. By choosing to include them you broaden your understanding of ideas about the self, knowledge and the world around us. Each book presents unexplored pathways into the study of world philosophies. Instead of privileging a single philosophical approach as the basis of comparison, each book accommodates the many different dimensions of cross-cultural philosophizing. While the choice of terms used by the individual volumes may indeed carry a local inflection, they encourage critical thinking about philosophical plurality. Each book strikes a balance between locality and globality.

Māori Philosophy is a first-person account of a philosophy for the Māori people. This is an introduction that brings to light a philosophical world in which its human and non-human inhabitants are held together in an intricate balance. It promises to significantly contribute to the making of a Māori identity, while simultaneously taking a stand on larger existential questions confronting our post-colonial, interdependent world.

—Monika Kirloskar-Steinbach

Finding Māori philosophy

The term 'Māori philosophy' provokes the meaning of 'philosophy' just as the phrase 'Māori science' – regarded by scientists as a 'contradiction in terms' – problematises the definition of 'science'. I began to think about the potential of Māori philosophy during my doctoral studies of Māori science curriculum (Stewart, 2007), since many accounts of 'Indigenous science' (also known as, for example, native science) seemed better suited to being described as philosophy, rather than science: frequently they exhibited apparent confusion between the 'facts' of science and the 'values' of Indigenous knowledge. I became interested in the idea that every form of knowledge, whether science, Indigenous knowledge, education, or whatever, has a theoretical base serving as its 'philosophy of knowledge' or epistemology, and the implications of this idea for investigating Māori knowledge. Almost every comparison between science and Indigenous or Māori knowledge I read seemed to miss this point: I found models with intersecting circle (Venn) diagrams and/or two-column lists of attributes, but very few comparisons between the philosophy of science and the philosophy of Indigenous knowledge. Attributes are surface features, but philosophy concerns the essence or nature of a body or form of knowledge – it is the ground on which that knowledge is built. To seek to understand the philosophy of any form of knowledge is to explore the boundaries between different forms of knowledge. This book contains an account of what I have found out by investigating these questions in relation to Māori philosophy, in and for education, broadly conceived.

The purpose of this chapter is to provide a brief introduction to the ideas that are central to this book. The section below gives a high-level conceptual definition of Māori philosophy. The following sections of the chapter explain aspects of the approach used in writing this book: its position in a book series on World Philosophies; the links between Māori philosophy and other intellectual traditions and fields of practice; a personal introduction focusing on my position in relation to Māori philosophy; the importance of te reo Māori (the Māori language) in this work; and a discussion of what I call the 'slippery path' between imperialism and romanticism. The chapter ends with a brief precis of the remaining six chapters.

Defining Māori philosophy

Māori philosophy is found in Māori discourses about the relationships between people, things, the environment and the world. Takirirangi Smith (2000) re-phrases the term 'Māori philosophy' as 'tangata whenua philosophy' and clarifies that by 'Māori' he means someone who can identify as tangata whenua through 'whakapapa kōrero'. Māori philosophy is therefore a central plank of identity for Māori people. Writing and reading about Māori philosophy are therefore politically significant activities. According to Smith, tangata whenua philosophy is made up of 'whakapapa kōrero' which are

• important narratives of identity;
• a knowledge base for the survival and welfare of the group;

- linked to major tribal artworks such as meeting houses;
- philosophical narratives invoked on important occasions to uphold the mana of the group; and
- discourses that rationalise existence through interconnectedness and identification of relationships between things that exist.
  (T. Smith, 2000)

Māori philosophy belongs to a different spatial and temporal reality from that of European philosophy. Time and space in Māori philosophy are unified: in the Māori language, separate words for space and time do not exist. Therefore, past events do not lose their significance, and ancestors can collapse the space-time continuum to be co-present with their descendants. The texts of pre-colonial Māori philosophy were found in the natural phenomena of 'place' as in ancestral localities of tribal occupation, interpreted through the senses, and recorded in human-made artefacts and taonga. Knowledge in Māori terms is not restricted to the physical senses, but includes knowledge obtained through intuition and dreams (C. W. Smith, 2000). This 'other' Māori reality has been marginalised and attenuated over time, but has never been fully stamped out. Being tangata whenua has meaning for a Māori person today, and one way of expressing that meaning is through Māori philosophy, as I will attempt to show through the chapters of this book.

Māori philosophy and World Philosophies: Writing this book

I understand 'World philosophies' as a descriptor or umbrella term for ways of thinking that arise from the cultures of the world's many Indigenous peoples, including Māori philosophy as a theorisation of Māori language and culture. World philosophies are inherently diverse; unified mainly by differentiation from global philosophy, which I understand as a term for the hegemonic Euro-American, or Western, modern, scientific underpinnings of knowledge. The tendency for terminology to keep changing makes it important to clearly define the meaning of these two important terms, and the difference between them, as I will be using them in this book. Particular care is needed to differentiate these terms for speakers of languages other than English (including the Māori language), in which the important nuances between the English pair 'world' and 'global' and between 'philosophy' and 'philosophies' may not carry over.

Global philosophy is singular, and the word 'global' is most strongly identified with globalisation, which is an inherently imperialist concept. The content of that which is described as 'Western' – whether in relation to philosophy, technology, culture or language – owes much of its meaning to the development of modern science, beginning in the era of the Enlightenment in Western Europe, whence the adjective 'Western' derives. In the twentieth century the centre of gravity of 'Western' culture shifted to the United States; today, in the twenty-first century, the power of wealth resides in multinational corporations, privately owned by uber-wealthy individuals. These individuals could be called 'global owners' with interests in all parts of the globe, including Aotearoa New Zealand, which has achieved some popularity in those elite echelons as a safe bolthole in the event of calamity in world centres. So the term 'Western' is no longer an accurate descriptor, and 'Euro-American' also has problems. The alternative modifier 'global' is more accurate; less tied to origins. The term 'global philosophy' then refers to ways of thinking that underpin contemporary 'global culture'. Nevertheless, the term 'Western' is widely used as the binary opposite of 'Indigenous' in relation to thinking, values, cultural preferences and so on, and this practice will be followed below, while remaining aware of the inherent limitations of the term. In my context, I usually refer to Pākehā-Māori relationships, but below I adopt the more general terms in referring to Western-Indigenous relationships, while cognisant that this term describes a reified binary, rather than a natural or scientific set of categories.

World philosophies is a plural term, and the word 'world', which is linguistically related to 'whole' and 'holism', has allusions of ecology and harmony with nature, which align well with Indigenous ways of thinking. The word 'world' draws our attention to the natural world, as against 'global' that calls to mind ideas such as 'the global economy'. Thinking about 'the world' is more likely to make us think of the image of planet Earth from space, with its marbled blue-and-white surface. One example of an international initiative using 'world' in this way is the World Indigenous Peoples Conference: Education (WIPCE) that has been held every three years since 1987, in venues rotating between the CANZUS countries (Canada, Australia, Aotearoa New Zealand and the United States), with the exception of the 2011 conference, held in Peru.

Since the 1950s, the development of Māori studies as a local form of anthropology in Aotearoa New Zealand brought Māori knowledge into the university curriculum, but in truncated form. In this process "Māori language and knowledge were re-framed as knowledge knowable from Western epistemologies" (C. W. Smith, 2000, p. 45). In the history of Māori studies, Māori philosophy has almost always been woven into the curriculum, rather than being seen as an identified topic. The Māori Renaissance, the recent emergence of Kaupapa Māori, and the growth of acceptance of Māori language and culture as part of general society, are aspects of an ongoing process of reviving and re-describing Māori knowledge, including the articulation of Māori philosophy. Māori philosophy research seeks to counter the Māori experience of colonization through history, which 'has involved a continual experience of decontextualisng and recontextualising the discourses of tangata whenua' (T. Smith, 2000, p. 54). This central technology of colonization is also described as 're-inscribing' tangata whenua discourse into Western knowledge.

Few Māori people have studied academic philosophy (I know of only two Māori with PhDs in Philosophy), and despite the strength of Kaupapa Māori education, very few Māori scholars have participated in the local sub-field of philosophy of education (C. W. Smith, 2000, p. 43). Despite the voluminous literature on all manner of Māori topics, no previous book with 'Māori philosophy' in the title was found at the time of writing (2020). This book stakes a claim for Māori philosophy in the emerging field of World philosophies, and provides an opportunity to re-frame and synthesise my body of work, sometimes pursued under other banners including Māori science education, Kaupapa Māori philosophical research and Māori education more generally. Understood in this way, a series on World Philosophies provides a convenient category and milieu for an introductory text on Māori philosophy.

I find it useful to regard Kaupapa Māori theory as a form of philosophy of education (Stewart, 2017b): a theoretical framework suitable for underpinning my practice as a critical Māori philosophical researcher. The researcher's identity is a matter of interest in any Māori research, including this attempt to provide an exposition of Māori philosophy. Some biographical detail about what brings me to this work is therefore warranted.

My right to write about Māori philosophy

I grew up in a bicultural Māori-Pākehā family in 1960–70s Auckland and received an excellent education in the state schools in Aotearoa New Zealand. With my family background of both my mother and her mother being teachers and avid readers, as well as poets, from an early age I enjoyed generous access to books, and reading was my first and abiding favourite activity or 'passion', as we would say today. So, teaching was 'in my blood', but it was not my first career choice, which was to help save the Takahē from extinction, after reading *Two in the Bush* by Gerald Durrell. When I left secondary school in 1978 that impulse saw me enrol in a bachelor of science degree at Auckland University, resulting in a first class MSc in organic chemistry in 1981. Following that I worked first as a research technician in the Cancer Research Laboratory in the Auckland Medical School, and later in sales and customer support of chemical analysis equipment.

At the end of 1988, I left my job and went north to live at Matauri Bay in an effort to reconnect with 'my Māori side'. From there I went further north to live with Mangu Awarau in Waimanoni, near Kaitaia, where I heard about Kura Kaupapa Māori, and extended my limited earlier knowledge of te reo me ngā tikanga (Māori language and customs). In 1991 I returned to Auckland and completed secondary teacher training at Auckland College of Education. After a year teaching te reo Māori at Onehunga High School, in 1993 I became the inaugural teacher of Pūtaiao (Science) and Pāngarau (Mathematics) at Te Wharekura o Hoani Waititi Marae in Oratia, Waitakere City, until wanting to live in Te Taitokerau (Northland) drew me to take up the Head of Māori position at Tikipunga High School in Whangarei in 1996.

My teaching and involvement with various national curriculum projects in Māori-medium education spurred me on to enrol part-time in doctoral studies in 2001 for a chance to investigate the Māori science curriculum. After graduating in 2007 I held short-term research positions before being appointed in 2010 as Lecturer in Education, University of Auckland, based at the Tai Tokerau campus in Whangarei. In mid-2016 I moved to my current academic position at AUT, Auckland, as an Associate Professor in the School of Education.

This book is an opportunity to re-frame and synthesise a set of ideas I have been thinking about since I began my doctoral thesis, almost two decades ago. Indeed, I seem to have been thinking about Māori philosophy for most of my life! I was an early observer when my wise old aunts and uncles made basic babyish mistakes in conversational English, such as saying 'him' instead of 'her'. Listening to conversations in Māori from under the hood of whatever car my dad and his mate were fixing made it seem natural to get up early to listen to the weekly Bruce Biggs Māori language lessons on the family radio in the sitting room. Likewise, the weekly *Listener* column by Ranginui Walker was household reading for years in my childhood home.

My focus in this book moves beyond the school curriculum to consider in more general terms how identifying as Māori and working with Māori knowledge influence one's everyday thinking and inform one's views on social matters of all kinds. In this book I present synoptic narrative accounts of central concepts and debates in

Māori philosophy in the form of a series of close readings of selected key texts and authors, interspersed with examples and vignettes from personal experience. The key texts and authors I call on are located across a range of fields: Māori education brings in Māori studies and anthropology, as well as sociolinguistics and some in other fields such as legal studies. I use Kaupapa Māori principles to guide a process of critically reading through and past the chauvinism of Eurocentrism and patriarchy found in most published work on Māori. I think of this approach as 'rehabilitating' older scholarship about Māori philosophy, for Indigenous purposes, under the wider umbrella of the Kaupapa Māori intellectual project.

Sources and links to social and intellectual history

One early way that Māori philosophy was inscribed in Western thinking was as religion, during the nineteenth-century European mission to convert 'native heathens' to Christianity – Anglican, Catholic, Wesleyan and so on. Hence Māori legal scholar Moana Jackson (1992) starts his paper on the colonization of Māori philosophy with the first words of the Bible: 'In the beginning was the word.' The process of colonization has included a sustained attack on Māori philosophy, and Jackson recapitulates 'what the introduction of an alien word has done to those words shaped in the kete of Tāne' (p. 1). The history of Māori colonization 'is a story of the imposition of a philosophical construct as much as it is a tale of economic and military oppression' (p. 2).

To research Māori philosophy is therefore by definition a political form of knowledge work: critical or Kaupapa Māori scholarship on Māori philosophy is necessarily activist scholarship, part of a process of reasserting and resurrecting subjugated knowledges, including those of Indigenous and non-Western peoples. This approach to Māori philosophy brings in Foucault's concepts of discourse and power/ knowledge, including his insights about identity, subjectivity and governmentality, and how language is used to construct and impose truth on the citizens of contemporary democratic countries such as Aotearoa New Zealand (Locke, 2004). As a philosophical form of research and scholarship, these alignments with Foucault mean that Māori philosophy also speaks to postmodernism and poststructuralism, and fits beneath the umbrella of Indigenous research based on post-colonialism.

Thus understood, Māori philosophy also shares common ground with the established tradition of radical philosophy, which is 'a collective body of work produced since the late 1960s by academic philosophers who seek to use their intellectual training and professional positions in the service of radical political, social, economic and cultural change' (Gottlieb, 1993, p. 1). This overview further explains that 'radical philosophers work and live in the three dimensions of the Western philosophical tradition, the counter-tradition of radical social theory, and the activist realm of political movements'. According to Gottlieb, Marxist theory and feminism play foundational roles in radical philosophy – we might consider them exemplars of the second and third dimensions, respectively, of radical philosophy. These dimensions form the grounds, theoretical and practical, on which to mount robust critiques of traditional philosophy. These links mean that Māori philosophy also shares commonalities with Marxist and feminist theory.

As already noted above, there is a voluminous literature on Māori topics: almost every imaginable Māori theme has been the topic of at least one book or article. The work of Elsdon Best, for example, is published under themes such as Māori knowledge of time, of astronomy, of the forest and so forth. From first encounters between European voyagers and tūpuna Māori (our forebears) a seemingly unslakeable thirst arose for all sorts of written material on everything Māori. Today, I see the same 'Māori knowledge' being applied in a range of disciplines: not only in education but also in health, business, justice and so forth. It is entirely understandable and to be expected that even Māori academics fall into line with Eurocentric institutional structures, including intellectual structures, but such work continues to read Māori knowledge through European categories. Indeed, I am inclined to think

ANY attempt to include Māori knowledge in the curriculum is bound to distort Māori knowledge.

'Māori philosophy' acts as a meta-theme or unifying category for a critical or Kaupapa Māori account of Māori knowledge, in seeking to counter atomisation across the disciplines of the university, the filtering of Māori knowledge through the domains of Western knowledge, and structures installed by 'global philosophy' and its academic systems.

The modifier 'Māori' disclaims expertise in the traditional discourses of academic philosophy represented in the national institutional milieu, very much like those of any other 'British commonwealth' country's university system. Detailed involvement in traditional academic philosophy is not important in my work, which derives from philosophy of education, not academic philosophy itself.

The use of 'philosophy' in the title indicates I am interested in Māori systems of thought about large existential questions, such as the nature of reality or the foundations of ethical practice. The use of 'Māori' also denotes cognisance that Māori philosophy draws on generalised and fragmentary accounts of traditional iwi (kingroup) knowledge – what Takirirangi Smith calls 'whakapapa kōrero' – that have long since entered the public domain. The utility of the term 'Māori philosophy' lies in its general applicability. As noted above, there is a place for Māori philosophy in World Philosophies, but Māori philosophy also aims to be useful to Māori political projects in a range of areas, mainly in tertiary education but with ripple effects into the community through domains of practice such as business, education, health and justice systems, media, and the government.

As explained in the first section of this chapter, Māori philosophy is treated in this book as a politically significant concept and topic. Māori philosophy is a response to over a century of colonization of Māori knowledge. The history of lack of Māori participation in institutional philosophy in Aotearoa New Zealand is not coincidental: the discourse of philosophy that underpins the entire (Western) academy has defined itself by excluding such forms of non-Western knowledge. The solution that emerged in the national academy was to inaugurate 'Māori studies' as a local form of anthropology, within which Māori philosophy is integrated, if implicit. About this history, Steven Webster writes:

Professor Ralph Piddington was the Foundation Professor of Social Anthropology at University of Auckland from 1950 to 1971, and established the first Māori Studies subject as well as the first Anthropology Department in New Zealand. (Webster, 1998, p. 103)

Webster goes on to trace the influence of this department under Piddington's leadership in producing generations of Māori academics, who along with their students have populated the departments of Māori studies around the country. He records how at Auckland, by 1993 Māori topics were being taught and Māori staff had been appointed in many faculties and departments across the university (p. 183), demonstrating the 'atomisation' process. But during the 1980s, coinciding with the introduction of neoliberal influences in state policy including education, the centre of gravity of Māori scholarship at Auckland shifted from Māori studies and began to also include Māori education.

The social movements of Te Kōhanga Reo and Kura Kaupapa Māori were bringing Māori adults back into education in unprecedented numbers, including in teacher training and academic education studies. Webster refers to the appointments in Education of Graham Hingangaroa Smith, Linda Tuhiwai Smith and Pita Sharples, despite their background in anthropology, as significant. These three were among the leaders of the struggle in the 1980s to establish the right for Kōhanga Reo children to attend Māori-medium schools (Reedy, 1992). With seminal local philosopher of education James Marshall as Head, the Department of Education at Auckland University at the time supported the Smiths, Sharples, Tuki Nepe and others to develop Kaupapa Māori theory as a form of academic intervention and a theory and philosophy of Kaupapa Māori education.

What we had in common was Māori knowledge and teaching. So we called ourselves Kura Kaupapa Māori ... [It] is primarily not a bilingual school or a total immersion school [but] a school which has a Māori philosophy as the most important thing. (Sharples, 1994, pp. 15–16)

These influences – philosophy of education and Kaupapa Māori education – are the major intellectual underpinnings of this work. My view of 'Māori philosophy' recognises the intercultural hyphen of the Māori-Pākehā relationship, a pervasive colonizing history which, as Moana Jackson (1992) points out, has operated at philosophical levels just as much as physical levels. In his paper Jackson assumes the existence of Māori philosophy, and traces the history of its oppression under colonization. Inspired by Jackson's seminal paper, this book takes the step of presenting an extended exposition of Māori philosophy, which aims to be both generative and teacherly.

Te reo Māori: The Māori language in this book

Despite the fact that this book is written in English, the reader must accept that te reo Māori, the Māori language, plays an essential role in Māori philosophy, and therefore in this book. I am writing in English but I am writing from a Māori point of view, and te reo is always important in my sense of a Māori point of view. I am writing in English but I am writing about Māori topics in which te reo is fundamental. Te reo Māori is the original language of Māori philosophy, and if the physical book were likened to its tinana (body) then te reo Māori would be its wairua (spirit). With whatever resources they have available, readers must imagine the stories and examples of Māori philosophy that are presented in English in this book as being conveyed in te reo Māori, the beautiful Indigenous language of Aotearoa, which developed in that land from the tongues brought across the vast ocean reaches, during the great migrations that peopled the Pacific in millennia past.

As foreshadowed above, te reo Māori text is treated as normal text in this thesis, since according to the Kaupapa Māori principles of the philosophy of this research, te reo 'is' normal, and the topic involves Māori-medium education. From my perspective this writing practice and research decision seem entirely unremarkable, but as a general academic practice it has only recently, and not yet universally, become acceptable to book publishers. In a text like this in which Māori words occur frequently it is the most practical formatting decision. It is also in keeping with the status of te reo Māori as an official language of Aotearoa New Zealand, and the reflection of this status in the importance accorded to the place of te reo in this work as the source language or 'mother tongue' of Māori philosophy.

One key textual practice is the strategic use of 'Aotearoa New Zealand' as the name of my country of origin, to highlight the bicultural framework of Māori philosophy. Māori words are translated (in brackets) or explained on first appearance. A glossary of Māori words follows the main text. Translations are mine unless otherwise noted, with Wiremu (Williams, 1971) being treated as the definitive reference for traditional words, and Te Taura Whiri i te Reo Māori (The Māori Language Commission, www.tetaurawhiri.govt.nz) as the authority for neologisms. Macrons have been added in quotes, particularly to prominent words such as 'Māori', and substituted for double vowels.

Technical details aside, the approach to te reo Māori in this book is in line with that taken towards Māori knowledge and Kaupapa Māori principles. This approach can be expressed as 'attempting to reverse the usual epistemological asymmetry' by which science/English is taken as the 'yardstick' of knowledge/language (Roberts, 1998, p. 69). The approach to te reo Māori in the text also follows the 'central tenet' adopted by Stephen May (2001) 'that the *normalisation* of minority languages within the public domain is a legitimate and defensible sociological, political and linguistic activity' (p.xiii, original emphasis).

Writing in English about Māori philosophy

The question of writing this book in English, or any language other than Māori, points to a deeper concern than publishing practices or making the text fully accessible to readers with no prior knowledge of things Māori.

> If colonization has caused views of creativity and creation to be anglicised and if the fundamental beliefs of Māori are gone, the

language becomes merely the translation of an English script. (C. W. Smith, 2000, p. 50)

This book is written in English, but Māori philosophy originates in te reo Māori, so the effect of translation between these two languages is important to consider. There are two language ideologies about translation in such situations, which can be clearly seen operating in Aotearoa New Zealand, in situations involving novel uses of te reo Māori in society. The first is an instrumentalist ideology, which sees translation "as a tool for transforming ideas into new linguistic patterns" (Blommaert, 1999, p. 13). This way of thinking about language reflects an overly technical way of thinking that sees a language merely as a code. In practice it assumes all forms of text can be unproblematically translated from te reo Māori into English, and from English into te reo Māori.

'The second one is a romantic ideology, in which language is an abstract idea inextricably linked with a people's "soul"' (Blommaert, 1999, p. 13). This language ideology is expressed in sayings such as 'ko te reo te mauri o te mana Māori' (the Māori language is the mauri, or life principle, of Māori mana) and 'ko te reo te kākahu o te whakaaro' (the Māori language clothes Māori thought). This way of thinking underwrites the central role played by te reo Māori in Māori identity. Te reo Māori and the English language are a real binary that sits at the heart of the national identity of Aotearoa New Zealand. Te reo Māori is the expression of the right of Māori people to be different from Pākehā. This language ideology opposes the idea that te ao Māori (the Māori world) can be fully and unproblematically translated into English. This idea that links a language to the 'soul' of a people explains why te reo Māori is such an emotional topic for Māori: for the language to die would feel like the death of the people. Since this book concerns itself with uniquely Māori ways of thinking and accounts of the world, and how these differ from what is currently considered 'mainstream' thinking, this second language ideology is important to the premise of this book. Te reo Māori holds the key to Māori philosophy.

I undertake writing in English about Māori philosophy as a bilingual and bicultural practice that aims for mutual respect between both languages and both cultures. I am a competent speaker and reader of Māori and identify as a Māori person, but think and write more fluently in English. In my writing I aim to foreground my Māori identity and experience through the personal details I share, the research choices I make, and the perspective from which I comment on larger issues. The concept of a 'Māori view' can best be understood as a relative rather than absolute binary, but nonetheless to assert its very existence challenges the philosophical universalism that underlies the entire (Western) academy, provoking us to think more deeply about much of what passes for 'common-sense' knowledge about the three philosophical questions this book explores from Māori perspectives: What is the 'self'? What is the world like? What is knowledge?

The slippery path between imperialism and romanticism

My invocation of the 'Māori perspective' is an attempt at 'both-and' rather than 'either-or' thinking. For me personally as a Māori scholar, this practice is an interpretation in my work of the 'two worlds' of Māori experience; my way of bringing forward my (Māori) being into my writing (C. Smith, 2000). As a bilingual Māori educationist with a science background, I subscribe to a 'de-essentialised' version of relativism that does not reject the basic tenets of epistemology, which are universal in human knowledge, but rejects the imperialism of what Western accounts traditionally do with those basic tenets (Herrnstein Smith, 2005). I accept the difficulty of dealing with the philosophical paradoxes thrown up by my doubled positioning, in seeking to capitalise on the productive tension of the binaries inherent in biculturalism.

In addition to the language binary represented by the role of te reo Māori in this book, there is a built-in binary in the logical premise of this book that influences its writing at every level. I refer to this binary as 'the slippery path between romanticism and imperialism' – a term warranting more detailed explanation, since it concerns an important question for this entire book project. To author an introductory text on Māori philosophy is, obviously enough, to stake a claim for the existence of 'Māori philosophy' – but this is not a straightforward knowledge claim. As noted above in the opening sentence of this chapter, the effect of the modifier 'Māori' in the term 'Māori philosophy' is to problematise the assumed range of meanings of the word 'philosophy'. I understand the term 'Māori philosophy' to be similar in scope to 'Māori thought' and 'an introduction to Māori thought' could have been an acceptable alternative title for this book.

The use of the term 'Māori philosophy' is deliberately provocative: it points to the political significance of the idea of Māori philosophy as much as it signifies a well-formed discipline or tradition. This point is underlined by the fact that when embarking on writing this book, I could find no existing book with 'Māori philosophy' in its title. My interest in writing about 'Māori philosophy' connects to my work on 'Kaupapa Māori philosophy of education' and Māori curriculum theory, which I understand as Māori philosophy in the sense of a theoretical framework for a field of educational practice: both theory and practice working together to resist and re-colonize the larger monocultural Eurocentric system, including the archives of scholarship on topics related to Māori philosophy.

The no-man's land from which I am writing lies somewhere between two theoretical positions: on one hand, there is the dominant tradition of Eurocentric accounts of Māori knowledge, thought, beliefs and philosophy, which analyses Māori materials – including texts – as objects of science, something akin to 'natural phenomena'. Anthropology: in the very name of the discipline is the trace of that imperialist history as Eurocentric knowledge of the Other. Māori have been studied by the edifices of science for well over a century, and continue to be studied on this basis by scholars all over the world. These studies have 'enframed' (Heidegger, 1977) Māori knowledge for non-Māori purposes. All of that history (past, present and future), and the way of thinking on which it depends, is summed up in the term 'imperialism'.

On the other hand there is the 'romanticism' of the culturalist tradition, which Webster in his 1998 analysis found was the major academic influence in Māori studies, and which has become further entrenched as orthodoxy in the intervening years. The culturalist tradition holds

> the ideological appeal of two worlds, and the Romantic inclination to identify 'the Māori world' with a functionalist or symbolic vision of a whole way of life rather than a critical history of a whole way of struggle. ... This escapism has been entrenched in Māoritanga since the 1920s, reinforced by social theories since then, and remobilised by opportunists in the Renaissance. (Webster, 1998, p. 188)

The last phrase refers to the recent uses of 'strategic essentialism' to help advance Māori political projects, a post-colonial term borrowed from Gayatri Spivak by Māori education scholar Te Kawehau Hoskins (2012). Taken seriously, this concept of 'strategic essentialism' points in the direction of a critical understanding of the limits of the romantic notion of 'pure' and 'authentic' Māori culture. Webster shows how romantic versions of Māori culture taught in university courses of Māori studies have become unhooked from the 'proletariat' life of material struggle lived by most Māori in the contemporary socioeconomic milieu. The imperialist 'standard version' of the national history of Aotearoa New Zealand cannot nourish the Māori intellect or soul, but neither can a romantic vision of a pure and untouched Indigenous culture.

Yet the Māori experience of 'living in two worlds' is genuine: it is not simply a figment of Māori imagination. Cultural difference is still on the loose in Aotearoa New Zealand: the spectre of a different tradition haunts the national imaginary. Perhaps what is important – and missing from the record – is the narrative that connects one to the other: an accurate account of the Māori experience of colonisation. If the shade could speak it would be in te reo.

Webster's gritty analysis is therefore a useful antidote to romantic ideas of Māori culture, which saturate discussions in those domains where Māori philosophy is applied, such as school curriculum policy, and education policy more broadly. Bicultural education policy has been used as a smokescreen in education policy in Aotearoa New Zealand for over thirty years to draw attention away from socioeconomic inequalities suffered by Māori, which are soaring along with the cost of housing in large centres, especially Auckland. Māori education including Kaupapa Māori education has capitalised on the opportunity those smokescreen policies have provided to establish their schools and other projects, but this does not mean that Māori-medium or Kaupapa Māori schooling holds the answer to overcoming every concern related to Māori education. All parties in these debates – researchers, community representatives as well as government actors – clearly must adhere to high standards of scholarship by acknowledging the diversity within Māori education, while not being taken in by ideologies, whether imperial or postmodern (which tends towards romanticism).

Māori families have absorbed a great deal of impoverishment over the last quarter-century, as capitalism has enriched its own by enforcing austerity on the already-struggling. Too many have broken down into violence, substance abuse and homelessness. But even in the most troubled suburbs and neglected rural areas of Aotearoa New Zealand, the strength of people working together and supporting each other keeps most of the population going on a more-or-less even keel, supported by the public health and education systems, which still work most of the time, amazingly enough.

The New Zealand Treasury brief to the incoming government of 1987 (New Zealand Treasury, 1987) included a chapter on Māori education that pointed out socioeconomic disparity did not account for all of the Māori ethnic gap in education outcomes. By a leap of logic the brief argued that education policy should therefore ignore socioeconomic factors in seeking to explain the cause of the ethnic gap. I would correct that lacuna and argue instead that *most* of the ethnic education gap can be attributed to the concentration of Māori in low socioeconomic brackets. I am interested in the 'extra gap' in education as one way of plausibly reflecting Māori 'difference' at an intellectual level – whether it be labelled symbolic culture, thought, philosophy or even 'native science' (Cajete, 2000). The realm of Māori philosophy lies in this occluded gap, this mental escape-hatch, this marginal liminal space inhabited in their thoughts by Māori people – to an outsider's eye, people indistinguishable from the non-Māori people with whom they freely mix in daily life. With other Māori, however, there are certain topics covered soon after first meeting, and mutual understandings that may never even need to be voiced.

The chapters to follow will return to these themes repeatedly, since they not only saturate the subject matter, but also dictate the approach taken to write about the subject matter. To unsettle the notion of philosophy in the guise of Māori philosophy is to straddle the philosophical abyss between imperialist universalism and romantic relativism, as outlined in the chapters to follow. I will not anchor my craft to either shore: better to stay adrift on the ocean currents in between.

Synopsis of chapters

The next chapter sets out brief definitions of some key theoretical ideas on which this book is premised. Following that are three chapters that deal in turn with Māori ideas about the self, the world and knowledge. Each of these chapters includes descriptions of fragments of traditional Māori knowledge, interspersed with examples from literature and personal experience, synthesised to build up rich, synoptic accounts on these central themes. Chapter 6 consists of examples or applications of Māori philosophy in writing about specific real-world scenarios. The short final chapter returns to the question of 'Māori philosophy' and the larger questions to which it connects in the past, present and possible futures.

Questions for discussion or research

- Investigate the uses of 'global' and 'world' as adjectives or modifiers in various contexts. Do your results support the argument in this chapter that 'global' is associated with capitalist power while 'world' is more fitting for Indigenous or folk values?
- Discuss the assertion that European colonisation of Indigenous peoples, including Māori, has involved philosophical subjugation, in addition to the more obvious physical aspects of colonising oppression. How does this idea link to that of 'epistemic violence'?
- Consider the premise that any attempt to describe a non-Western philosophy such as Māori philosophy will run up against logical conflicts.

Theoretical concepts for researching Māori philosophy

To inform my research into Māori philosophy I draw on a set of key ideas originating mostly in linguistics, anthropology and sociology, and various off-shoot disciplines such as cultural studies, Māori studies and Māori education. In borrowing from across the disciplines in this way I see my background discipline of education more like a filter across the disciplines, rather than a discipline in itself, giving rise to sub-disciplines, including philosophy of education, history of education, sociology of education and so forth. The purpose of this chapter is to list and briefly annotate some important theoretical concepts, which are applied in various ways throughout the remaining chapters. The order starts from the general and basic and proceeds towards the more specific, applied or elaborated concepts.

Weak relativism

The very idea of Māori philosophy raises a serious challenge to the universalism inherent in Western knowledge. Weak relativism refers to the universalism–relativism binary and comes first in this list because it is the most fundamental level of the binary underpinning Māori identity, the ground on which each of the following concepts rests. Universalism is a cognitive value and philosophical commitment that is central in Western knowledge based on the universal application of the laws of science – in other words, acceptance that the laws of physics and chemistry apply at all times in all places, while the laws of biology could be said to apply in all settings on this planet.

The universalism–relativism binary is a reified pair of oppositional philosophical concepts, often presented in cartoon or 'straw-man' versions, even within the academy. Any challenge raised to the dominance of the scientific view beyond its brief is seen by the incumbent power bases as anti-science, or equated with creationism (or religion, superstition, etc.). I have never read or heard of an Indigenous author who denies these basic laws of science, the three-dimensional reality of the natural world and its physical boundaries. Rather, an Indigenous scholar (me, for example) objects when science transgresses beyond its bounds: as the old adage goes, when 'is' becomes 'ought'. If science is factual, objective and value-free then how can it evaluate its own worth as a knowledge system?

I follow Barbara Herrnstein Smith (2005) in seeking to de-essentialise the way the concept of relativism is used in these debates. A challenge to universalism does not have to ignore the basic laws of science, in seeking to unsettle and shift the monoculturalism and Eurocentric ideologies that have been extrapolated from these debates, as they apply in my local context. My right to identity as Māori ultimately depends on acceptance of cultural difference. If it is not to be reduced to merely a brand in the marketplace, my identity as Māori must be accepted as implying a philosophical position of limited or weak relativism.

Weak Sapir-Whorf theory

The Sapir-Whorf hypothesis (Lee, 1996) was a modern re-statement in the 1930s by Edward Sapir (Sapir, 1933) and Benjamin Whorf (Whorf, 1956) of a fundamental idea about the relationship between language and thought. In its strongest interpretation the Sapir-Whorf hypothesis was taken as a claim that language determines thought, a position also known as 'language determinism' and one that has since been conclusively disproved by empirical investigations, in favour of the notion of 'universal grammar'. The alternative interpretation is known as weak Sapir-Whorf, or 'language relativity', and holds that a natural language influences and is influenced by the thought patterns of that language, which taken together form the worldview of that culture. Whorf's ideas were ahead of their time: his work with Hopi and other Indigenous languages led him to develop a critical multicultural research paradigm and ethics, through which he articulated an early version of the poststructuralist concept of 'discourse' that today is attributed mainly to Foucault (McHoul & Grace, 1998). The celebrated sociolinguist Joshua Fishman revisited the Sapir-Whorf hypothesis (Fishman, 1960, 1980) and in the 1980s proposed a third 'globalised' version of Sapir-Whorf: ethnolinguistic diversity as a worldwide cognitive asset for humanity (Fishman, 1982).

Worldview theory

The worldview concept was heralded by and within the debate about philosophical relativism and the Sapir-Whorf hypothesis at a time when the modern Western academy had amassed a great deal of information about many different cultures, languages and knowledge bases, based on primary anthropological field studies. The term 'worldview' is an English version of the German word *Weltanschauung*, traced back to Kant who seems to have coined it in his 1790 work,

Critique of Judgement, to mean how one sees the world in terms of sense perception. The worldview concept gradually spread across the emerging social sciences in the twentieth century, developing and changing to mean how one understands the world. Distinction has been made between two levels of meaning of the worldview concept – one philosophical and one cultural. The terms 'articulated worldview' and 'lived worldview' were assigned to these two levels of the worldview concept. 'In any given cultural setting, the distinction between the two is often obscured, provoking endless headaches among scholars' (Cobern, 1991, p. 17).

Critical theory

Critical theory is an academic tradition attributed mainly to the Frankfurt School, a German philosophical tradition started in the 1930s with leading names including Max Horkheimer, Theodor Adorno and currently Jurgen Habermas. Critical theory challenges the universalism and Eurocentrism of science and the overall modern Western academy. It is difficult to interpret critical theory into an applied field like education, which is expected to be normative in the sense of didactic, yet must also be open to difference in order to fulfil the larger educational aim of helping the student to go beyond the teacher.

The differend, incommensurability and epistemological diversity

The differend is a concept from the work of French poststructuralist philosopher Jean-Francois Lyotard (1988) and refers to the 'gap' in understanding between two or more different worldviews, which applies when comparing a Euro-American against an Indigenous worldview. The gap between Pākehā and Māori worldviews serves as a good example of how this concept works. The differend is a reminder that two worldviews may begin from different underlying frameworks, hence languages may not be fully translatable in the final analysis. This 'gap' in translation can also be expressed as a 'deferred' meaning, in which multiculturalism either remains beyond the bounds of the possible or is incorporated into practice in truncated, tokenistic ways.

Incommensurability is another term for the 'gap' in understanding between two interlocutors: it is a contested term in philosophical debates because it depends on acceptance of epistemological diversity, which leads back to the dreaded relativism (Hoyningen-Huene & Sankey, 2001). Epistemological diversity and hence the universalism–relativism binary are also important in the debates about Māori science, which have been mostly in relation to public science spending, the environment, and science education for Māori students including reo Māori science education (Dickison, 1994; Lomax, 1996; Peters, 1993). In my doctoral study I combined the two concepts of 'Kaupapa Māori' and 'Māori science' to produce 'Kaupapa Māori science' (Stewart, 2007), which is a critique of science guided by Kaupapa Māori theory and research principles including a basis in Māori philosophy, space for te reo and tikanga Māori, and being motivated by Māori interests and perspectives.

Cultural hybridity, third space and liminality

Cultural hybridity is another concept borrowed from biology and applied to bi-, multi-, cross- or intercultural contact and mixing via ongoing relationships, such as sharing in one country and society. As a metaphor it may be harmless, but its links to notions of genetics and 'breeding' have made this concept especially unpopular among post-colonialist scholars and minoritised peoples. The same idea is perhaps more insightfully expressed by Homi Bhabha (2009) as the 'third space' which refers to a productive outcome of fruitfully combining elements from more than one culture. In this conceptualization, applicable to the

Māori context, the first space refers to the autochthonous whole culture prior to contact; the second space is under erasure, at the subjugated minoritised margins of society in what is often called the colonial era; but the third space uses the productive tension of cultural contact and interaction to create new, unanticipated cultural forms and products. The creative potential of interculturalism is clearly seen in the cultural and bicultural history of creative arts in Aotearoa New Zealand, including music and movies.

These cultural patterns bring in the idea of knowledge boundaries or borders, giving rise to further elaborated notions of marginality, liminality and border crossing, in relation to biculturalism and cross-cultural relationships and products. Liminality is similar to the third space as a theorisation of cross-culturalism. The concept of cultural liminality as a strategy for openness to the future of humanity is most famously associated with the name of symbolic anthropologist Victor Witter Turner (1920–83).

Kaupapa Māori theory

Kaupapa Māori theory is a strategic intellectual intervention against the Eurocentrism that pervades research, education and the academy. Kaupapa Māori theory originated in the discipline of education as a theorisation of Kaupapa Māori education, and a theoretical framework for Māori research and practice. Since its origins, Kaupapa Māori theory has been extended and more generally applied across many social science domains. It has also served as a paradigm for new forms of research that are Māori-centred in terms of the questions asked, why and how the research is undertaken, and the motivations and processes at each stage of research, from initial planning to dissemination of the results.

Kaupapa Māori theory serves as a philosophy of education to guide how research is thought about, which is known as Kaupapa Māori research methodology (Pihama, Cram, & Walker, 2002; Pihama, Smith,

Taki, & Lee, 2004; S. Walker, Eketone, & Gibbs, 2006). Every way of doing research has its strengths and weaknesses, and collecting empirical data by conducting interviews or surveys is not the only type of research project, though it dominates the field in educational research. Policy documents, research literature, media, general literature and original narratives are other sources of data for Kaupapa Māori investigations.

Questions for discussion or research

- What is 'scientism' and what are its various forms? Discuss possible examples of how scientism operates in society and in academia.
- Does science as a knowledge system contain inbuilt paradoxes and limitations? How does the concept of 'scientism' relate to this question?
- Discuss and define the links between the concepts of

  worldview,
  relativism,
  incommensurability, and
  differend.

- Are the above four separate concepts, or is it more accurate to think of them as different levels or versions of the same concept?

3

Still being Māori

Chapter outline

Māori ideas about the 'self'

Hūtia te rito o te harakeke
Kei hea te kōmako e kō?
Kī mai ki ahau, he aha te mea nui o te ao?
Māku e kī atu, he tangata, he tangata, he tangata

This well-known proverbial saying from the people of the far north of Aotearoa refers to the flax plant growing outwards from the centre – a favourite Māori metaphor for the human family (whānau) as a unit of society. Māori customs for harvesting the flax, an extremely valuable material resource in Māori culture, use the terms child, mother, father for the inner trio of growing leaves that should never be cut, lest the plant die. Only the 'tūpuna' or 'ancestor' leaves are harvested, just as

Figure 1 Harakeke flax plants in flower (photograph taken by author, 2015, Matauri Bay Northland, Aotearoa).

old people are taken by death, separated from their living kin, to realms beyond everyday reality.

If the flax plant should die, asks the saying, where would the bellbird sing? The bird's song is a metaphor for Māori symbolic culture: the genres and repositories of cultural narratives and oral histories that inform all Māori concepts and understandings of relationships and identities, philosophies and technologies. The final two lines of the saying mean 'if you ask me what the most important thing in the world is, I will tell you it is people, it is people, it is people'. The beauty of the flax plant (harakeke or kōrari) in full bloom is portrayed in Figure 1, and its cultural centrality is celebrated in this poem.

Harakeke

Roots clustered, entwined in the body of Papatūānuku
In slow searching plant time, patiently growing
Seedheads leaning, reaching upward to Rangi
Gathering light and air, sunshine and strength
Into fibres for the scraping, the soaking, the rolling,
Delicate golds and halftones of different green
Humble colours, not dazzling like scarlet kaka feathers
Not striking like the bright plumes of kotuku or hawk
But homely, strong as a woman built for childbearing
Provider of warp and weft, the fabric of being.

Wharikitia te whare mo te manuhiri
Kia pai te whare mo te manuhiri

The house must be prepared to welcome the manuhiri
The whariki woven and spread, life is the guest –
On the whariki we were conceived and born, and there we slept
Feeling it firm beneath us, sheltering and warm.
The whariki supported our coupling and when life was spent
There we were laid to be mourned, our spirit farewelled
At the last we were wrapped in a whariki, returned to Earth.
Season succeeded on season, dark followed light
Unblinking eyes of our foremothers gazed to the future
To us their descendants, knowing their strength was sufficient
Despite betrayal for guns, death in the swamps
Bequeathing a cloak to cover us, a kete for treasures.
We are part of the pattern that must never be broken
We must continue the weaving, even the bruised ones
Our work will fashion the nets to catch the stars.
  – Trixie Te Arama Menzies (author's late mother) in *Uenuku*
(Menzies & Maihi, 1986, p. 13)

Māori ideas of the self as captured in traditional oral texts such as the proverb discussed above recognise a part of the human being that exists in addition to the physical body. This 'supernatural' part is called the 'wairua' which is most commonly translated as 'spirit' – indeed 'waitahi' is an old word for the body, for which the dominant word used today is 'tinana'. 'Who' in Māori is 'ko wai' suggesting 'wai' has a meaning related to 'personal identity' so waitahi and wairua can be rendered as 'first part' and 'second part' of the person. This binary model of the Māori self approximates to equating the waitahi with the physical body and its functions, and the wairua with the psyche/soul and its symbolic products. The pair of words 'waitahi' and 'wairua' as well as the phrase 'ko wai koe' suggest that the word 'wai' (common meaning 'water') had metaphysical levels of meaning associated with identity, that is, whakapapa and the binary nature of the human being, physical and psycho-emotional (or spiritual). Likewise, the word 'hau' (wind) had metaphysical levels of meaning related to spiritual forces, as in the examples 'hau taonga, hau ngāhere, hau kāinga, haututu, hauora' (Stewart, 2017a).

The Māori language does not contain gendered pronouns, and traditional texts do not contain references to the superiority of men or the subordination of women. In Māori philosophy humans contain two components: te ira atua, obtained from the realm of Ranginui, and te ira tangata, the component obtained from the earth mother Papatūānuku. Individuals who on conception receive slightly more of te ira tangata turn out to be females while those who received an imbalance of te ira atua turn out to be males. 'Males are represented generally as expendable and are employed in all the risk-taking activity' (T. Smith, 2000, p. 57).

Māori ideas of the 'self' imbue every part of being Māori in thought and action, such as talking to one's dead, and an elaborated set of ideas around kinship that direct Māori interactions. For example, when a group approaches a place that is 'tapu' (taboo or under restrictions) such as a whare (meeting house) where the deceased is lying in state, old women will call out in greeting. These traditional calls are addressed to the ancestors that Māori believe are carried along (in wairua form) with the living people. They are calling to that part of the human being that transcends the physical dimensions, as well as time and the death of the body. Another saying from the people of the far north is the phrase 'koutou kua whetūrangitia' – addressed in the second-person plural to the once-living ancestors, 'you who have become stars'. I learned these Indigenous Māori ideas by word of mouth, handed down in oral traditions from the elders of the taumata, the speaking positions of the marae or traditional community centres of iwi or kinship groups of the far north, from generation to generation, without intermediary non-Māori structures such as school or book.

This, then, is 'pure' Indigenous knowledge, or as close as one might get to it today – an idea discussed further in the following two chapters. As often happens, the holistic nature of Indigenous knowledge runs into conflict with the categories of 'philosophy' (noting that the unmodified word 'philosophy' is usually understood as referring to 'Western philosophy') and the structure that organises a book into chapters – in this series, chapters on the self, the world and knowledge. For this reason, it will be necessary to cross-refer between these chapters. One of my aims below is to point out examples of everyday 'factual knowledge' or 'common sense' about Māori identity that turn out to be based on Eurocentric myths or ideologies, distortions of science, in particular the regimes of evolutionism, which are central in the edifice of scientific racism upon which New Zealand was first established in Aotearoa.

Certain common sense 'facts' taught for generations at primary school in New Zealand, such as the division of Pacific peoples into Polynesian, Melanesian and Micronesian, fall apart under closer scrutiny. Māori and Pacific traditions provide different ideas. There are well-established traditions of pre-European inter-island traffic, trade and intermarriage between Samoa, Tonga and Fiji. This Indigenous knowledge contradicts the 'common-sense' European science classification of Indigenous Fijians as Melanesians, and people from Samoa, Tonga and Rarotonga as Polynesians, along with Māori. The same Eurocentric attitudes that underpinned racist Victorian-era science are implicated in the current treatment of the island nations of the Pacific as little more than holiday destinations in mainstream Aussie and Kiwi culture. In the same way, the existence of Māori as an Indigenous culture in Aotearoa New Zealand is erased from the accounts told by non-Māori that make up the national imaginary of the dominant culture.

Māori origin stories

Māori traditions are structured by a corpus of originary and nature narratives that reflect the underlying concept of kinship between human beings and all the rest of the elements of the natural world in which we live. The cosmogenic narratives of how the world came into existence are presented and discussed in the following chapter. Māori philosophy also incorporates more local originary stories, in line with the understanding of Māori knowledge as a form of Indigenous knowledge, which is place based and does not make assumptions about its own generalizability. When we consider more local texts of identity it becomes relevant to pluralise the discussions, since the stories vary from place to place. Rather than Māori philosophy we might prefer to talk of Māori philosophies, then perhaps take the next step to tribal philosophies, since the term 'Māori' itself is a generalization – an ethnicity rather than a tribe.

In my own case, on my father's side I come from the northern part of the North Island of Aotearoa. Māori know the North Island as Te Ika a Maui, and the northern tip is Te Hiku o te Ika, the tail of the fish. Northland more generally (from Auckland north) is Te Taitokerau, the 'northern tide/coast' – Māori spatial concepts for the points of the compass being organised around coastal direction. There is a significant oral text from the north known as Te Whare Tapu o Ngāpuhi, the sacred house of Ngāpuhi (see below – this version is personalised to my own maunga or mountain, Whakarārā). Te Whare Tapu o Ngāpuhi starts with lines that mean 'my house is built with Ranginui as the roof and Papatūānuku as the floor; the poles of the house are the following mountains.' It then names the major peaks that encircle Ngāpuhi territory (in modern terms from Whāngarei in the south to Kaitaia in the north) thus delineating the homelands that 'house' the people of this kin group in its larger sense, known as Ngāpuhi-nui-tonu. This oral text contributes to a sense of belonging to the kin group or iwi identity of Ngāpuhi, whose genealogy is still widely retained and actively maintained.

Te Whare Tapu o Ngāpuhi

He mea hanga tōku whare, ko Papatūānuku e takoto nei te paparahi,
ko Ranginui e titiro iho nei, te tuanui,
Ko ngā poupou o te Whare ko ngā rārangi maunga;
Whakarārā titiro ki Tokerau,
Tokerau titiro ki Rākaumangamanga,
Rākaumangamanga titiro ki Manaia e tū kohatu mai rā i te ākau,
Manaia titiro ki Tūtemoi,
Tūtemoi titiro ki Maunganui,
Maunganui titiro ki Pūhanga-tohorā,
Pūhanga-tohorā titiro ki Te Ramaroa e whakakurupae ake rā i runga,
Te Ramaroa titiro ki Whiria, ki Te-Paiaka-o-Te Riri, ki Te Kawa-o-
Rahiri.
Whiria titiro ki Panguru, ki Papata, ki Te Rākau-patapata e tū ana ki Te
Hauāuru;
Panguru, Papata titiro ki Maungataniwha,
Maungataniwha titiro ki Tokerau,
Tokerau titiro ki Whakarārā.
Ēhara aku maunga i te maunga nekeneke,
ērangi he maunga tū tonu, tū te ao, tū te pō.
Ko te Whare Tapu o Ngāpuhi tēnei,
tihei mauri ora.

There is no question of claiming title to all or even any of the lands delineated in oral texts of identity such as *Te Whare Tapu o Ngāpuhi*. The Māori sense of belonging to particular places, captured in the word 'tūrangawaewae' or home ground, is neither cancelled out nor reversed by legal ownership in Pākehā terms. To understand oneself as originating from this land, belonging to these hills, valleys, rivers and coasts, and as kin to all their inhabitants, is a powerful antithesis to the individualistic notion of the human being that has overtaken the world along with Euro-American culture under globalisation. Being Māori in 2020 is many different things, at different levels, to different people. But one simple way to express a general characteristic about what 'being Māori today' means – perhaps the most central unifying concept for all Māori – is to acknowledge that Māori have unique origin stories and histories, which are fundamentally different from those of white or settler New Zealanders, known as Pākehā.

Māori ethnicity

Early European travellers in Aotearoa in the late 1700s to early 1800s called the Indigenous people 'New Zealanders' but according to standard reference works (Williams, 1971, p. 179) the label 'Māori' (with a capital M) had come into general usage for this purpose by around 1850. To whom the label 'New Zealander' referred gradually changed in the early decades of the nineteenth century, as Europeans began to be born in New Zealand and to identify as being from New Zealand; indeed, even today, many white New Zealanders self-identify as 'New Zealand Europeans'.

With a small 'm' the word 'māori' has a traditional meaning of 'ordinary' – for example, 'wai māori' means drinking water and 'wai tai' means sea water. The coining of 'Māori' as a general label for the Indigenous peoples of all the tribal groups throughout Aotearoa is an example of the classic process of ethnicity formation, understood as arising from contact between different cultural groups, and being made up of various different aspects (Eriksen, 2002). For Māori ancestors, the British invasion and settlement of Aotearoa was a confrontation with cultural difference significant enough to catalyse a new ethnic identity as tangata Māori (Māori people). The Māori identity adds to, rather than replacing, traditional tribal or kinship group identities. The Māori identity is a self-consciously modern collective concept: in many ways it is the outward or Pākehā-facing side of Māori identity, beyond which Pākehā seldom glimpse. As a collectivity it makes sense to speak of being Māori in the singular – 'a' Māori identity – while tribal identities, as noted above, are more adequately discussed in the plural.

Tūhoe elder John Rangihau (1992) demonstrates this twofold nature of Māori identity in his piece *Being Māori* published in the classic collection edited by Michael King *Te Ao Hurihuri*, which was first published in 1975. Rangihau addresses his 'identity and commitment to Māori things' but as he gets into the details he turns to speak about his 'own tribe, Tūhoe' and the specific experiences he took part in to teach the tribal culture to the younger urban generations, who were losing their links to their history, language and land. When giving specific detail he speaks about Tūhoe things, but his general commentary is about 'the Māori world' (Rangihau, 1992, p. 187), even using the anthropological singular, 'the Māori': 'down through the centuries the Māori has been very close to nature' (p. 187). He comments on how his experiences in the Māori Battalion during the Second World War gave him a strong sense of citizenship as a New Zealander, and his disappointment on his return that 'we were still treated as second-class citizens, where we were still not allowed to purchase alcohol and where we had to get Polynesians or Indians to do this for us' (p. 187).

Rangihau writes about being unable to book hotel accommodation in a number of New Zealand towns in 1957 'purely and simply because I was Māori' (p. 188). From this point he begins to reflect in more negative terms about attitudes, which cannot be legislated against, and the pressures he felt the dominant culture exerted on Māori to become Pākehā, to adopt Pākehā culture and values. 'The Māori is content to stand right where he is, retain his culture and retain his identity, and be himself, not a foreigner, in his own country' (p. 189).

> Although these feelings are Māori, for me they are my Tūhoetanga rather than my Māoritanga. My being Māori is absolutely dependent on my history as a Tūhoe person as against being a Māori person. It seems to me there is no such thing as Māoritanga because Māoritanga is an all-inclusive term which embraces all Māori. (p. 190)

Throughout his paper Rangihau describes what it means to be Māori, using the hybrid word 'Māoriness' rather than 'Māoritanga' as in the sentence, 'They [Tūhoe] had managed to retain a little more of their Māoriness than others' (p. 184). It is an authoritative and nuanced reflection on various levels of identity, their intersections and politics – as Tūhoe, as Māori, as New Zealander. His final paragraph issues a bleak warning and a focused critique of the term 'Māoritanga':

> I can't go round saying because I'm Māori that Māoritanga means this and all Māori have to follow me. That's a lot of hooey. I have a faint suspicion that Māoritanga is a term coined by the Pākehā to bring the tribes together. Because if you cannot divide and rule, then for tribal people all you can do is unite them and rule. Because then they lose everything by losing their own tribal histories and traditions that give them their identity. (p. 190)

The identity label 'Māori' is a modern ethnicity initiated by contact with difference: therefore, by definition, it emerged post-contact with Europeans, while by contrast the iwi or tribal kin groups existed before contact. This point was acknowledged by American anthropologist Allan Hanson (1989) in his controversial article, *The Making of the Maori: Culture Invention and Its Logic*. In this article Hanson offered a non-Māori view on 'Māoritanga' or Māori identity, from the other end of the spectrum to Rangihau. Hanson intended to self-critique his own discipline of anthropology by pointing out that cultural patterns described in the anthropological literature, such as the whānau-hapū-iwi model of Māori society, were often cartoon versions or 'constructions' of the actual cultural situation, which was always more complex and dynamic than the academic analysis. But the politically inflammatory way this article was taken up by the public media eclipsed its potential scholarly value; this article and its story have become a legendary episode in the colourful history of Māori ideology in the academy.

Hanson described two such 'invented' Māori traditions: The Great Fleet theory of Māori settlement of Aotearoa and the 'Io cult' that Hanson sees as a post-contact modification of the Māori cosmogenic narratives. The public media seized on Hanson's claims and used them as 'proof' for the favourite Pākehā myth of 'no more real Māori' (discussed in detail in the following sections). Indeed, Hanson's article could be read as saying that 'Māori culture' was invented by academics, raising (for anti-Māori interests) the question of whether there ever had been any 'real Māori' at all!

Yet Hanson in his famous article seemed to confuse the two concepts of Māori/iwi culture and ethnicity, outlined above. Māori culture exists in Indigenous iwi (tribal) traditions, independent of academic studies, and subject to ongoing adaptation as conditions change. Māori *ethnicity* is a pan-tribal identity that coalesced in response to colonisation. So, the Māori identity is a 'placeholder' or generic form of the multiple 'tangata whenua' cultural identities that reside among the iwi (kin groups or 'tribes'). The way iwi identity underpins Māori identity is obvious to Māori, but not necessarily to non-Māori, not even to 'scientific' authorities such as Hanson. The Māori identity works in much the same way as the concept of 'Indigenous' – it is a placeholder term for diverse specific traditions that are localised and place based, unlike each other, but sharing a philosophical base that remembers what global Euro-American culture has forgotten, and a similar political history of struggle to survive against the 'fatal impact' of European colonization (Moorehead, 1968).

Hanson's delineations of what Māori are and what they think are two-dimensional cartoon versions that lack the depth offered by Rangihau. Hanson actually references Rangihau's paper (the 1975 edition), but only to support his point that 'Māoris are no longer willing to tolerate being told by Pākehās what is good for them, and even how to be Māori' (p. 894). Ironically, when the Māori elder Rangihau wrote in 1975 that Māoritanga was invented by Pākehā, it raised no eyebrows; but when the US expert Hanson published the same claim as research fourteen years later it unleashed a media frenzy!

Hanson's article lends substance to the 'suspicion' expressed by John Rangihau that Māoritanga was a concept invented by Pākehā to 'unite and rule' Māori. For example, Hanson comments in detail on the *Te Māori* exhibition, dubiously describing it as 'one of the most effective projects to publicize Māoritanga's invention of Māori culture' (p. 896). He fails to mention that *Te Māori* was funded by Mobil (Rau-Kapa, 1993), and overlooks its enormous economic value to the New Zealand brand in the emerging global market. *Te Māori* is a classic example of how Māori and Pākehā motivations can be completely different and yet converge and work together to pull off something spectacular.

Though his article debunked the authenticity of contemporary ideas about Māori traditions, it presented a cartoon version of modern Māori identity. Thus Steven Webster, another American anthropologist studying Māori, criticised Hanson's analysis, calling it essentialist, and accusing it of failing to escape the circularity of cultural relativism (Webster, 1998). Hanson's conclusion adopts a form of postmodernism that loses sight of power, hence letting go of reality. Hanson takes an auto-turn in commenting on the article as an artefact as he writes it, calling it a 'sign-substitution' and part of an 'invention of tradition' literature. The self-conscious tone of this section clashes with the ambiguous neutrality of the rest of the article. It ends with this final paragraph:

> To acknowledge the presence of inventions in anthropology may appear to jeopardize its capacity to locate truth and contribute to knowledge. But that would be to miss the point of the entire argument. It would assume the existence of some other form of discourse that trades in fixed rules and eternal verities – in short, that logocentrism reigns. The thesis of this essay is that invention is an ordinary event in the development of all discourse, which therefore never rests on a permanent foundation. From this point of view truth and knowledge stem – and have always stemmed – from inventions in the decentered play of sign-substitutions. (A. Hanson, 1989, p. 899)

The problem here is that the word 'inventions' in the first sentence undercuts Hanson's conclusion that a 'new idea' or 'novel insight' counts as an 'invention' in anthropology, and reverts to the sense of 'inventions' as being distortions and fabrications, such as the Great Fleet or Io cult. This confusion confounds the inattention to the question of 'who paid?' for *Te Māori*, overlooking *economic* discourse, which does in fact 'trade in fixed rules', namely, the rules of the global financial markets.

This article (Hanson, 1989) is an interesting example of the genre of academic literature about Māori culture, written by non-Māori authors, which typically uses 'Māori' as object of study – an example or context for their topics. There is no evidence that Hanson paid attention to possible negative effects his article could have for others, including Māori others. Such lack of ethical care in research on Māori was part of what necessitated the invention of Kaupapa Māori theory (Smith, 1997), as further discussed in the following chapters.

Webster re-tells the story of the 'Hanson affair' provoked by this article, using it as a data source in his own analysis of postmodernist Māori politics (Webster, 1998, pp. 229–36). History gifts us such controversies as case studies of the intercultural relationship between Māori and Pākehā. Records of who said what, why and with what effect are traces of the discourses of ethnicity. Webster's account of this affair is part of his larger project to record the intellectual history of Māori studies at the University of Auckland.

Webster describes how the Hanson article hit the media in Aotearoa New Zealand shortly before the start of the 1990 academic year, and gives an account of a 'panel discussion' held at the anthropology department at Auckland, a few weeks later, in which he participated, along with Graham Smith (2003), Rangi Walker (1989) and Anne Salmond (2012) (Webster, 1998, p. 233). He records how Salmond and Walker both 'criticised Hanson for failing to understand Māori culture' (p. 233) while he and Smith 'in different ways emphasised the one-dimensional or depoliticised character of Hanson's analysis' noting as reassuring that 'the theoretical split crossed the Māori/Pākehā lines of the panel' (p. 234). Webster recapitulates Hanson's argument about the 'invented' nature of 'Māoritanga' and concludes:

> I myself do not find this a satisfactory solution to the dilemma [of how anthropologists can be taken seriously if they have actively participated in the 'invention' of a culture] because it is circular. One basis of this circularity is the assumption that a culture is discrete and homogeneous. Which bearers of which culture? Which heritage (if all are illusory)? Who (which anthropologist? which native leader?) says 'they' accept it, and which 'they' is meant? That is to say, we are back where we began, in the ambiguously circular reasoning of doctrinal cultural relativism [which] assumes *a priori* systems of essential meanings to begin with.

> I would argue that the beginning point is instead necessarily a specific history and a specific situation in which some systems of meaning are supported and others undermined and a culture is a continuous whole only ideologically. A people probably make or construct a

culture much as they make history. However, quite unlike in Hanson's and other meanings-based and often voluntarist views, they don't make or 'invent' it just as they please, but under conditions which are historically given. (Webster, 1998, p. 231)

Webster posits two contrasting notions of Māori culture – this ideological version 'in the illusory but reassuring sense of "a whole way of life"' that he discerns entraps Hanson as well as Salmond, Walker and the 'culturalist' tradition, as against the reality of Māori identity and culture that is impossible to capture in such written works, which Webster terms 'a whole way of struggle' (p. 225). The verb 'struggle' lends this term a more agentic and politicised sense of Māori identity, in contrast to the dusty museum or exalted art gallery images of 'Māori culture' that populate the national (Pākehā) imaginary. The term 'a whole way of struggle' is apt insofar as to be Māori in the contemporary milieu is to identify with being on the subaltern side of the racist colonizing binary of Aotearoa New Zealand history.

Only European (Pākehā) New Zealanders have the (white) privilege of being able to ignore the racialised nature of society in Aotearoa New Zealand. To identify as Māori is to stand up for cultural difference; to raise a small protest against the universalism and inhumanity of the contemporary global culture. Māori people often say they live in 'two worlds' – a sense that arises from the fact that Māori have to live with the cultural binary. The point is that however a Māori person chooses to navigate this cultural binary, navigate it they must.

Cultural difference in the contemporary world-system

Identity difference and diversity is costly in terms of business models, which forms the basis of the rationale in economistic terms against the idea of cultural difference.

The Western world is today dominated by the political power of the United States, and that power is associated with an economic system which stretches its organising, purchasing and marketing mechanisms all over the world. In that endeavour, the standardisation of demand is of considerable advantage to the huge multinational companies, and there is therefore a lot of money riding on the elimination of troublesome differences between cultures. (Willmott, 1989, p. 2)

In the framework of ideas that underpins the global economy today, all cultural difference is reduced to choices in the marketplace: all human values are brought into the ambit of the global profit machine. Māori culture and identity are 'consumed' by this profit machine and recycled as brand. In Aotearoa New Zealand, the past three decades of neoliberal-style economic policies have begun to dismantle the social welfare system, while simultaneously priming the urban housing market, resulting in the current despicable problems of child poverty and homelessness, of which Māori and Pacific families are bearing the brunt (Carpenter & Osborne, 2014).

To identify as Māori today is to be aware of the extent to which Māori are problematised and demonised in the state apparatuses. To the extent that the Indigenous Māori sense of cultural difference resides in the symbolic realm, it is invisible to outsiders and therefore discounted. It is therefore understandable that Pākehā struggle to see, let alone understand, the Māori point of view. There is a tendency for Pākehā to see Māori only in relation to their own interests. Education policy for Māori is an example of how this works: the addition of Māori culture into the school curriculum has been justified on the grounds of its benefits for Pākehā children (Smith, 1986). Today, difference is about all that is left for Māori to claim: the alternative history that informs contemporary Indigenous Māori identity. Māori material and symbolic territory has been taken over and brought under the Pākehā regimes of bureaucracy, legality and privatisation. Health, welfare and justice systems, aided by schools and other education institutions, control the lives of most Māori people today. Only that which lies beyond the reach of money cannot be alienated from Māori.

What lies beyond the reach of money is the realm beyond the physical, beyond the quantitative: that which makes us truly human, otherwise expressed as the wairua, the second part of the person. This part of being human is expressed through dialogue and through love – two important modes of human-level praxis that money can never trump, since even death cannot destroy the power of ideas, or the power of love. Naturally, the enormous private profit machines that currently direct humanity's activities exploit these practices and their underlying theoretical frameworks to the fullest extent to which they are capable. The point for Māori philosophy is that it is in dialogue, and in love, that the individual human remains in control of one's own decisions: even in the limited forms of democracy now seen in the countries of the former British Empire, to the extent that they can withstand the pernicious effects of advertising and other propaganda industries, each person controls the content and tenor of their own utterances, and the passions and commitments of their own hearts.

Being the 'other': A politicised self, a mythologised self

As the 'Hanson affair' demonstrated, Māori culture and identity are politically contentious, and of constant interest to local non-Māori news media, who are susceptible to carrying distorted and sensationalised accounts that have been found to be anti-Māori (Moewaka-Barnes, Borell, Taiapa, Rankine, & McCreanor, 2012). Occasionally, items of pseudo-history, based on white fantasies of overturning Māori claims to indigeneity, have been reported as fact (see Hamilton, 2017). The following two examples show how when Māori object to Pākehā stereotyping as racist, Pākehā claim satire or humour ('tongue-in-cheek' suggestions) or accuse Māori of infringing their democratic rights to free speech. In May 2013 the publication of two newspaper cartoons, one shown in Figure 2, by award-winning cartoonist Al Nisbet, generated criticism by various Māori politicians, as well as Susan Devoy, the then human rights commissioner (Radio New Zealand, 2013).

In the context of rapidly rising rates of homelessness and child poverty, primary schools in low socioeconomic areas (invariably those with high proportions of Māori and Pacific residents) were setting up

Figure 2 Cartoon published in *The Press* (Christchurch) newspaper, 30 May 2013.

'breakfast clubs' in efforts to equip children to come to school ready to learn. Devoy expressed distaste for the cartoons but advised they did not breach the Human Rights Act. The cartoonist Nisbet expressed surprise at the negative reaction evoked by his images, which he said were aimed at those who complained about being poor but who smoked, drank and gambled. Māori Labour MP Louisa Wall took the case to the Human Rights Review Tribunal, but it was eventually dismissed (Wright, 2017). This incident catalysed another round of the free speech debate in relation to an image such as a newspaper cartoon, a genre with a rationale and a long tradition of social and political satire and critique.

Even more recently, just before Waitangi Day in early February 2018, local business tycoon Sir Bob Jones came under fire for a piece published in his regular column in the well-regarded *National Business Review*, in which he proposed a 'Māori Gratitude Day' on which Māori would serve Pākehā, 'bring us breakfast in bed or weed our gardens, wash and polish our cars and so on, out of gratitude for existing' (The Spinoff, 2018). The negative reaction incited by this article prompted the paper to remove it from its website, after which both Jones and the paper claimed to have ended their relationship. In response to his article, Māori filmmaker Renae Maihi collected over 65,000 signatures on a petition in an unsuccessful bid to strip Jones of his knighthood.

Since Pākehā commentators have dominated channels of communication for most of the history of the Māori-Pākehā relationship, certain Eurocentric myths and ideologies have become embedded in the common-sense knowledge on which these ethnicity debates turn. This imbalance has begun to be reversed in recent decades, with the setting up of Māori media outlets, including community radio stations, as well as greater Māori presence in the academic institutions and literatures that support public media, but the dominant myths and stereotypes show little sign of being dislodged, as the Jones example shows.

One key Pākehā myth about Māori is that there are 'no real/full-blood Māori left', which was the assumption Jones took as 'undeniable fact' to give a point to his satirical proposal about Māori 'gratitude' to Pākehā for their non-Māori heritage. Even if the notion of 'no real Māori' were to be accepted as factual, his reasoning is still specious in suggesting that individual Pākehā, such as himself, are somehow identifiable with any and all Pākehā ancestors that a particular person might happen to count in their family tree. The point is it is entirely reasonable that Jones should believe the myth to be literally true, since distorted versions of national history have been taught to school children in New Zealand for many decades. Indeed, I recall being taught this 'fact' myself as a ten-year-old child at school in Auckland in the early 1970s, despite knowing that my paternal grandmother was alive and well at the time, and that she was widely acknowledged and accorded status for her pure Māori lineage.

Someone who does not know many Māori people well (such as Jones, perhaps) would have no basis in direct experience to counter the myth. I personally know enough full-blooded Māori people to believe there are many still alive today; but the dominance of the myth is counterfactual, which makes it difficult to mount a credible counterargument. To Māori, full Māori whakapapa can increase a person's mana (prestige), but conversely to have non-Māori ancestry does not make a person any less 'Māori'. My grandmother inherited significant lands through her whakaheke rangatira (chiefly descent lines), and I was told her arranged marriage to my grandfather, who was of mixed Scottish/English and Māori heritage, was seen by her mother as being beneath her, in Māori social terms. The 'no full-blood Māori' myth operated in inverted form in my own family history.

Longstanding liberal attitudes towards intermarriage in Aotearoa New Zealand play a role in supporting widespread belief in the truth of this myth, since a significant proportion of Pākehā people have a Māori connection somewhere in the wider family. The 'no real Māori' myth is a prime example of a Eurocentric ideology that works to reinforce a sense of Pākehā security and superiority in relation to Māori. A classic example of its use in this way is in the frontispiece Raymond Firth used in his major book *The Economics of the New Zealand Māori* (Firth, 1972), shown in Figure 3: a

Plate 1   Frontispiece   R. A. Falla
THE PASSING OF THE OLD ORDER
Waewae Te Kotahitanga of Ohawa-te-rangi with the spear and cloak of former days

Figure 3 Photograph of Waewae Te Kotahitanga, Frontispiece in *Economics of the New Zealand Māori*, by Raymond Firth (1972).

classic Māori portrait of the early modern era of an unhappy-looking man standing in front of a building made using European materials, and dressed in European clothing, but 'with the spear and cloak of former days'. Centred directly under the photograph appear the words 'the passing of the old order'. The tone is one of eulogy and admiration, typical of such scholarly writing on Māori, and indeed to be expected in any study requiring such dedication and intense interest.

The point being made by the choice of both image and words, however, is that Māori power is dead, which is, of course, a requisite for eulogy. This demonstrates how the underlying purpose of the 'no real Māori' myth is to resign 'real' Māori culture and identity to the dustbin of history. This ideology is consistent with the politics of 'smoothing the pillow of a dying race' (Stenhouse, 1999, p. 85), which dominated race relations, from a Pākehā viewpoint, following the end of the New Zealand Wars from about 1890 (with the exception of the armed attack on Rua Kenana's stronghold at Maungapōhatu in 1916, see *Te Ara – The Encyclopedia of New Zealand*, 2018b). Even the received view of population trends, in which the Māori population is widely considered to have declined to a nadir of about 40,000 in 1896, before recovering again in the 1900s, is suspect when placed under the logic microscope of ontology. Who was counting in 1896, who was being counted, and what criteria were used for classifying individuals as Māori or European? What it means to be Māori has changed continuously through the years. Today, self-identification is the accepted norm for determining ethnic identity in Aotearoa New Zealand, but it is far from clear that the same views were held in a census conducted in the colonial milieu at the dawn of the twentieth century.

The ongoing appeal to the myth of 'no real Māori' is testament to the influence that social Darwinist beliefs retain in Pākehā and mainstream thinking (*Te Ara – The Encyclopedia of New Zealand*, 2018a). This myth sits within a constellation of mutually reinforcing ideas, including that Māori were conquered in war, and as losers lost all rights; that Māori gave up their sovereignty in signing the Treaty of Waitangi; that Māori were not the first settlers of Aotearoa, so cannot claim rights as first peoples; that Māori were an inferior type of people compared to Europeans, with inferior intelligence, language, technology and culture; and that only intermarriage with Pākehā had 'saved' Māori, with the concomitant result that no real or 'pure' Māori remained alive, in any case.

Distorted versions of history, biology and social science, mixed together with ignorance and arrogance, make a formidable basis for white privilege in Aotearoa New Zealand, despite the generally genial nature of everyday inter-ethnic interactions. According to this thinking, Māori were lucky to have received the benefits of European colonisation, and anyway, since it all happened a long time ago, Māori today need to 'get over it' and get on with it. These mendacious historical residues embedded in national discourse (such as school lessons) have been reinvigorated by recently implanted neoliberal ideas, which equate wealth with virtue and hard work, and blame the victims of economic restructuring for being lazy or making 'bad choices'. About a year before the column discussed above, Sir Bob Jones was reported as saying that beggars in Aotearoa New Zealand were usually 'fat Māoris' (The Spinoff, 2018) and were a 'disgrace'.

This section has dug into the dominant distorted Pākehā views of Māori: the chapter concludes with the next section based on a Māori perspective of the same question, including personal narratives and histories.

Fractions of Māoriness – family skeletons

People do not live their lives in fractions. In the first post-contact generations, the children of Māori women who were used to entice a Pākehā settler, which was a great asset to the iwi in the early days, or who worked as ship girls in the era of international sailing ship trade, grew up in Māori communities and were culturally Māori. To base concepts of Māori identity on blood quantum arguments is an appeal to the outdated concept of 'race' that was ejected from the lexicon of science many decades ago, and replaced by ethnicity, which arises through difference, and draws on both primordial definitions, including whakapapa, and situational definitions (Eriksen, 2002), including choices made by the individual – as Hanson put it, 'making a conscious choice to practice the tenets of Māoritanga'.

The following story about fractions is a personal anecdote of identity but paints a picture of a kind of family history that is a reasonably common experience in Aotearoa New Zealand, which is founded on the historical relationship between Indigenous Māori people and white settlers predominantly from the UK. My mother passed as Pākehā but was 1/16 Māori, the fifth female in a maternal descent line back to my ancestress Merekaimanu, who links me to Rangi Tōpeora, the subject of one of the classic Lindauer portraits of the 1800s (Auckland Art Gallery Toi o Tamaki, 2018). In marrying Merekaimanu, settler Edward Davis acquired her ancestral land interests, and prospered. The family settled in Cambridge, Waikato, their home being the large villa Val-Mai, today offering bed-and-breakfast-type accommodation. As the years went by, detailed knowledge of the Māori heritage was suppressed in the family. Generations later, about the only residual acknowledgement of the Māori ancestry was in the form of a racist, patriarchal, science family myth. The story, as told to my siblings and me, was that when in the 1930s our mother's father had asked for our grandmother's hand in marriage, he was warned by her father of mental instability in the women of the family, caused by the Māori blood. The 'mixed blood' was a useful explanation of past family tragedies including illness, depression and even suicide. With scientific overtones, it subscribes to a proto-genetic framework of understanding of identity. It suggests belief in a fundamental physical difference between Māori and European people involving the 'blood'. This was considered 'good science' at the time.

To say 'my mother was 1/16 Māori' illustrates how 'fractions of Māoriness' were the terms in which ethnic identity was spoken about in my childhood family, living in the worst house in the street so as to be just inside the Grammar Zone – the area of Auckland where children could by right attend the city's most prestigious secondary schools. One of my clearest childhood memories is of a family discussion about 'how much Māori' we were. My father counted himself three quarters Māori, so from him we were 3/8. Adding on the 1/32 from my mother, we decided we were 'three-and-a-bit eighths' or 'just under half'. It was a potent fractions lesson: right away I resolved to myself that I would 'marry a Māori' so my children would not again have their 'blood' halved. Decades later, my two siblings and I have all had children with full Māori partners.

Sir Bob Jones would probably splutter at this claim, but while it might at first sight seem provocative and counterfactual, in terms of Māori identity as ethnicity rather than as 'race' it is a straightforward and entirely reasonable assertion. To give up the pseudo-science of a genetic understanding of 'race' is to change the focus for assessment of ethnic identity. If one's four grandparents all self-identified as Māori and conducted their lives according to that understanding, one is fully Māori. By this criterion my father was full Māori – certainly he could not see himself as anything but Māori, and his parents and the other adults in his life as a child were all Māori in language, culture and subjectivity.

In re-framing the question of being Māori today as one of ethnicity, it becomes unnecessary to hold Māori to the higher of a double standard of complete knowledge of one's genealogy, as in the following example. The myth of 'no full-blood Māori' has featured in the political career of Don Brash, who in 2006 recalled the 1989 Hanson affair when in his 'Orewa speech' he questioned the status of Māori as an ethnic group on its basis. In response, newspaper reporters were despatched to track down a 'pure' Māori – and my friend Mangu was the first and closest one they found, under treatment at the time at Auckland Hospital. The article shown in Figure 4 was published in the *New Zealand Herald*, complete with a tightly cropped mugshot, even cutting off his ears, as shown by comparison with the original photo (Stokes, 2006). The cropped image has an eerily dehumanizing effect that can only be deliberate. This editorial act objectifies the face, presenting it trapped

Full-blooded challenge to Don Brash

BY JON STOKES
MAORI ISSUES REPORTER

PATRICK Flonce Rivers seems an unlikely name for a full-blooded Maori.

While family and friends know him by his Maori name, Mangu Awarau, it was from English with a touch of French that the parents of the former boilermaker/welder chose his name.

The 57-year-old father of eight now lives in Waimanoni, north of Kaitaia, where he grows organic kumara and peruperu.

He was bemused to read comments by National Party leader Don Brash questioning whether Maori remain a distinct indigenous group because there are few if any full blooded ones.

"So he thinks I belong in a museum?"

On the day of the interview, the Ngaitakoto hapu member is in Auckland awaiting surgery for **Mangu Awarau** the cancer which has ravaged his body for six years.

He is one of 14 children. Just four brothers still survive.

While their unblemished Maori heritage was known in the Waimanoni community, it made little difference to how they were treated.

"We were ordinary Maori like everyone else in our neighbourhood. It's still the same now. I don't look at them and think they are quarter-caste or half-caste. They are whanaunga [relatives], just like me. I don't think I am anything special. If Don Brash thinks I am special, good for him."

As a child he was desperate to be known by his Pakeha name, at a time when being Maori meant you were nothing.

He railed at the name Mangumangutaipo (since shortened to Mangu), loosely translated as "black demon", given by an uncle.

Being Maori has little to do with blood purity, he says. It is determined by whakapapa, and upbringing.

"I have a nephew and niece who have blond hair, blue eyes, some who are half-Samoan, some Dalmatian. They are Maori, and they are whanau."

Figure 4 Photograph of Mangu Awarau published in *NZ Herald* newspaper, 30 September 2006. Left: The photo as it appeared in print. Right: The photo as it appeared on the newspaper's website www.nzherald.co.nz/nz/news/article.cfm?c_id=1&objectid=10403690.

in a box like a specimen, reinforcing the suggestion in the article that it 'belongs in a museum'. The dramatic emphasis in the brief text on Mangu's illness also seems suspect – as if hinting at the old evolutionist spectre of biological inferiority.

Mangu was able to provide testimony to contradict the claim that no full-blood Māori remain alive. Knowledge of one's whakapapa remains important and still widespread in Māori society today. Someone who is sixty today only has to go back to grandparents or great-grandparents to reach the time before intermarriage was fully acceptable (in either Māori or European terms). If there are no non-Māori ancestors in those generations, as is the case for Mangu, and my paternal grandmother, then the claim to being full blood must be considered literally true. But of course, one counterexample does not call the myth seriously into question. As a social 'truth' that plays an important role in supporting Pākehā feelings of security and superiority, it has a counterfactual power, resistant to reason, that can only be described as ideological.

Māori identity is at its base an ethnic self-concept, and ethnicity choices available today in Aotearoa New Zealand are probably about as diverse and liberal as they have ever been, anywhere. My mother, despite her Māori ancestress, grew up as a Pākehā, but chose to explore her suppressed Māori heritage. My father, despite his British ancestor, grew up as a Māori, internalising various negative stereotypes. In the newspaper article Mangu pointed out that although his cousins could boast a Pākehā ancestor, while he and his siblings could not, they all considered themselves 'equally Māori'. In the contemporary era, complicated and mixed self-concepts of all kinds have become socially accepted, but in past generations social choices were more restricted, and ethnicities correspondingly simpler. My father's grandfather was an example of this: born in the 1850s, he was the youngest of four boys, the children of a Māori mother and a Pākehā father (the Stewart ancestor), who plied a trade in kauri timber for housing across the Tasman Sea, between Northland and Sydney. When their father left Northland for the final time, the two older boys went to live with their paternal uncle and grew up as Pākehā men, while the two younger brothers, including my great-grandfather, stayed with their mother and grew up as Māori.

The history of Aotearoa New Zealand society boasts an enormous range and quantity of intercultural possibilities for making families and happy marriages, especially since the Second World War, to a greater extent and in a safer environment than in most other places. We could imagine other plausible national 'truths' – for example, 'no full-blood Pākehā' – and reflect on the potential of such a change on the national psyche. Such 'thought experiments' bring into focus the strategic, ideological nature of this truth-myth in the discourses of nation-building. As with the Great Fleet and other anthropological inventions, Māori as well as Pākehā have learned this myth at school, and Māori have reached the point today that few individuals have the luxury of both time and records to piece together alternative Māori narratives in the numbers that would be required to seriously overturn it.

We do not need to go to the atomic level to find science, or to compare truth claims in Western terms against those of Māori knowledge. But convincing comparisons between the two forms of knowledge must accept the cognitive values of both. This narrative has investigated the accepted 'fact' that no full Māori remain, and has compared it with an Indigenous perspective. The question left to hang is this: which knowledge claims in this narrative count as 'good science'?

Questions for discussion or research

- Discuss the difficulty of labelling any aspect of Indigenous knowledge or experience as 'pure' or 'authentic' in the contemporary milieu, and how this conundrum can be navigated in studying world philosophies.
- Indigenous peoples in modern Western societies, such as Māori people in New Zealand, suffer from being both romanticised and vilified in public discourse such as the media. Find and discuss some examples of both these opposing attitudes towards Māori and/or other Indigenous groups.

Te ao Māori – the Māori world

Māori ideas about 'the world'

For tangata whenua [there] are two clearly identifiable realities. First, the reality of colonisation, or being Māori in a Pākehā world. ... But there is also another world view which occurs in another spatial and temporal dimension which is not that of European or Western notions of time and space. (Smith, 2000, p. 60)

Three beliefs implicit in Māori philosophy that have been omitted from the curriculum are:

1. Everything in existence is related.
2. All things are living.
3. Worlds regarded as 'unseen' in Western terms can be mediated by the human. (T. Smith, 2000, p. 45)

Karakia [incantations or 'prayers'] are metaphorical doorways that allow access to other realms. Doorways have guardians who can allow or deny access – hence the importance of the doorway of the house. Certain creatures such as owls, bats and lizards were considered 'guardians of the spiritual realm, intermediaries between the living and the dead'. (Smith, 2000, p. 46)

When we express our identity we do so in relation to a concept of the world in which we live, so Māori ideas about the world were bound to impinge on Māori ideas about the self as discussed in Chapter 3. Māori people often report their experience as 'living in two worlds' and these worlds are named as te ao Māori (the Māori world) and te ao Pākehā (the Pākehā world). Other pairs of terms to express this binary are 'te ao tawhito' (the ancient world) and 'te ao hurihuri' (or 'te ao hōu', the changing world, the new world); 'nō neherā' (from a long time ago) and 'nō nāianei' (these days); 'i mua/muri i te taenga mai o te Pākehā' (before/after the arrival of Pākehā).

Although the colonisation of Māori meant their insertion as a population into the lower brackets of the emerging economy, the ruling powers never totally obliterated Māori culture, so the Māori world (which we might call Aotearoa) has remained alive on New Zealand society's margins, in pockets far from the nation's urban centres and power suits. Thus, under the bed or on the top shelf of the wardrobe, families keep their taonga (valuables, heirlooms) such as kākāhū or korowai (cloaks, typically woven from harakeke with entwined bird feathers) and pukapuka (whakapapa books). There is nothing fake about Māori life on the inside, and these sorts of examples defy Hanson's (1989) and others' delineations of 'Māoritanga' as 'invented' culture.

Māori people, like other Indigenous peoples, continue to explore the possibilities offered by culture, wherever they find themselves in the changing social milieu, from the cataclysms wrought by the arrival of Pākehā down through the generations to the contemporary technological age. In this sense what is meant by 'the Māori world' keeps changing. We can understand the phrase 'te ao Māori' in two senses: first, as a 'traditional Māori world' frozen in time by Pākehā invasion, which does not change, and second, as the Māori world experienced by today's generations, which continues to evolve under the influence of everything that has happened since its collision with the Pākehā world. To define Māori ideas about the world, therefore, both of these senses must be included, in order to present a Māori-centric account that disrupts dominant Eurocentric traditions, which have interests in promulgating notions of Māori as a 'dying race' and the Pākehā habit of calling time on the Māori world.

In my experience, Māori people generally do not claim literally to believe the ancient Indigenous nature narratives rather than the cosmological accounts of contemporary science. On the other hand, in some big central ideas the Māori accounts of the world make more sense than science or modern capitalist ideas. Relatedly, Māori ideas of the world are valuable sources of values based on a virtue ethics of ecology and community (Patterson, 2000). The Māori genealogical model of the universe has been studied by science for close to 150 years, since the first recordings of Māori knowledge by pre-1900 colonial anthropologists including Elsdon Best, Percy Smith, John White and others. Māori re-readings of this kind of work show how Māori ideas about the world were distorted, leading to serious misreadings (Stewart, 2017a).

More than this, there is a 'truth about stories' (King, 2003) that is of a different order from scientific truth. This form of truth is more vibrant and apparent in Indigenous narratives and metaphors in comparison to contemporary mainstream discourse, based on received accounts of science. Current research on narrative theory is challenging long-held dominant ideas about cognition and knowledge (Herman, 2003), and narrative methods are finding more acceptance in qualitative research (Chase, 2013). This truth about stories shines from the Māori creation stories, which besides anything else are simply good stories, and have been retold countless times. Below is my synopsis of some of the creation stories or cosmogenic narratives that go to make up the Māori genealogical model of the universe (one standard book version is Alpers, 1996).

The geneaological Māori universe

At the heart of the Māori world is Papatūānuku, the primordial mother earth deity. Above is Ranginui, the primordial father sky deity. Their many children are guardians of various domains, including Tangaroa, god of the sea, Tāwhirimātea, god of winds, Haumiatiketike, god of wild foods, and Rongomātāne, god of cultivated food, especially kūmara, hence 'god of peace'. Tūmatauenga is god of war, but the most important brother for humans is Tānemahuta (also known as Tāne, or sometimes Tāne-nui-a-Rangi), ancestor of mankind and all the trees, birds, insects and other land animals and plants. It was Tāne who managed to separate their parents in the first place, to end their millennia-long tight embrace, with all their children crouched in the dark between them, and allow the light of day to enter the world. Tāne planted the trees of the forest, and filled them with the birds and other living things. Tāne cloaked his father Ranginui with the night sky, adorned it with the stars, and begat humanity with Hineahuone, the primordial female ancestor god, whom he fashioned from clay. Tāne ascended to the heavens and returned with the three baskets of knowledge for humankind. The rain is likened to the tears of love from Rangi to Papa, and the mists her sorrowful sighs in return. The youngest unborn brother is Rūaumoko, god of earthquakes and volcanoes. When he moves inside his mother's belly, the earth shakes and rumbles: perhaps in the twenty-first century his time draws near?

These narratives have been published in English many times over since people first started writing books on Māori topics, which was soon after European contact with Māori and has carried on since, still showing no sign of stopping. In that sense they have long since passed into the public domain of social discourse in Aotearoa New Zealand. Of course I did not first learn them at the knee of an elder around the metaphoric hearth – rather it was from a favourite childhood book (the classic *Wonder Tales of Māoriland* authored by A. W. Reed), a Christmas gift to me and my siblings from our non-Māori maternal great-grandmother. Over the decades I have seen and heard numerous versions of these Māori creation stories: they have been published in books of all kinds, including children's reading books and educational materials. They have been televised, presented in plays, songs, artworks, exhibitions and of course online. These narratives describe the Māori genealogical model of the universe, which underpins any discussion of Māori knowledge, worldview, paradigm or philosophy.

The above paraphrasing is just a taster of the Māori creation stories that continue down through many generations to result in the world around us, an idea that makes sense from a local Māori or (more correctly) iwi perspective, referring here to the world as the physical geography or natural environment making up the traditional homelands of one's people, connected through to the micro-level, such as delineated in Te Whare Tapu o Ngāpuhi in the previous chapter. The hills and waterways of one's ancestral home area, known in Māori as one's tūrangawaewae (literally place to stand), are part of the body of Papatūānuku, who is our ancestor. Plants and animals are the descendants of Tānemahuta, from whom people also descend, according to Māori ideas about the world.

Māori ideas about the world thus centre on whakapapa, a word whose nearest English equivalent is 'genealogy', although whakapapa has a wide range of meanings and allusions not applicable to genealogy, and is also used as a verb. Whakapapa is a master concept in Māori philosophy because it not only structures the content of knowledge about the world (beginning with the creation stories and continuing to include all the physical elements of the natural world) but also provides an ethical framework based on kinship with/in the world. Whakapapa both explains the world and guides human behaviour in the world. Whakapapa and the genealogical model of the universe provide a theoretical underpinning of the Māori values, based on ethical concepts of ecology and community. Whakapapa is how Māori people introduce themselves to each other and how they understand other people – a major topic of Māori conversation.

In traditional Māori thought, whakapapa was graphically represented in carvings 'as a double spiral marked by chevrons to show successive epochs' (Salmond, 1985, p. 247). The spiral form of whakapapa is associated with the idea of growth and development over time (as in the fern frond) and is a major motif in Māori iconography. The whakapapa concept is also a record of the passage of time, based on the imprecise unit of a generation. In a society organised along communal kinship lines, knowledge of whakapapa had both social and economic value. If whakapapa measures time, the spiral notation of whakapapa reflects a Māori notion of time as cyclic, rather than the Western concept of linear time. The conceptual importance of whakapapa is returned to in the following chapter on Māori knowledge.

The Māori creation stories, or nature narratives, are therefore both theories about reality and philosophies that give rise to ethics and values to guide behaviour. The Māori nature narratives are known throughout scientific and Anglophone literary accounts (what is known in Māori as 'te ao Pākehā' meaning 'the Pākehā world'). At a philosophical level, the whakapapa kōrero (T. Smith, 2000) of the genealogical universe provide an explanation of the world and natural phenomena; in other words, taking the role now played by the central concepts of science, in providing an underpinning theoretical framework for all empirical Māori knowledge. Almost all published comparisons between science and Indigenous knowledge fail to allow for the fact that science consists not only of detailed empirical knowledge and knowledge criteria, but also of an underlying theoretical model of the universe (a philosophy of science) that gives rise to both criteria and content of science knowledge. Without this understanding that a knowledge base has philosophical, theoretical and empirical levels, most published comparisons between science and Indigenous knowledge are fatally flawed.

Anthropologists and other scholars dismissed the Māori genealogical model of the universe as 'fireside tales' (Firth, 1972, p. 150), which they disconnected from empirical Māori knowledge about the environment that they were seeking to put on record. Elsdon Best (2005), for example, made extensive studies of Māori forest lore, yet seemed unable to make the connections between Māori practice and Māori theory, leaving him famously puzzled about the hau of the forest and the 'hau of the gift' (Stewart, 2017a). Unfortunately, such mistakes are embedded in mainstream Western scholarship about the Māori world, with ongoing influence seen today in the contemporary efforts to 'include' Māori knowledge in curricula, policies, research and so forth. The next chapter on Māori knowledge considers these themes in more detail.

The dipolar Māori cosmos

As well as being based on a genealogical or whakapapa model of reality, te ao Māori is a world of binaries or polarities that operate at many different levels, from cosmic through to the everyday physical dimensions, to psychological, spiritual and philosophical levels. I liken these binaries to 'dipoles' in a metaphor from chemistry that refers to the dynamic separation of electric charge in an overall neutral molecule. In anthropological analyses these Māori binaries have been called 'dualities' and characterised in terms of 'complementarity' and 'symmetry' (F. A. Hanson & Hanson, 1983). This binary nature of Māori reality is similar to concepts found in other Indigenous models, such as Yin Yang, the basic Taoist concept that goes across many dimensions from physical (e.g. nutrition) to philosophical. Given the current archaeological explanation of the ancient peopling of the Pacific, including eventually Aotearoa, from Taiwan as a jumping-off point, it is unsurprising to find alignments between Indigenous Māori concepts and those of ancient Asian philosophical traditions. The 'dipolar' metaphor captures the sense of two complementary opposites that are separated yet joined, and that neutralise each other's energies.

The Hansons (1983) studied Māori in the classic structuralist traditions of anthropology, which although since destabilised remain a major source of dominant ideas, within and beyond the academy. Anne Salmond (1978) achieved a more nuanced and useful delineation of the dipolar Māori cosmos by using a semantic approach to anthropology, in which 'the Māori language itself is the main line of evidence, rather than reports by European observers as to how they viewed Māori custom' (Salmond, 1978, p. 5). Salmond depicted a cosmos structured by foundational 'oppositions' (p. 7) or poles (pou), formed by pairs of attributes including ora/mate (life/death), tapu/noa (sacred/profane), ao/pō (day/night) and many others. I imagine these pou as arranged like the spokes of a spinning bicycle wheel, which serves as a metaphor for the spiral nature of time in Māori philosophy. The area in between the ends of the pou, represented by the hub of the bicycle wheel, is the pae – 'the threshold, liminal zone that mediates the main oppositions' (pp. 15-16).

The word 'pae' or 'paepae' has a range of literal meanings relating to 'edge' ideas including horizon, circumference and horizontal beam. In the dipolar model of the Māori cosmos the pae is the zone of life, in which humans have moral agency to exercise will and act in the world. Salmond describes the central importance of the pae in Māori ideas about the world:

> The activity here [in the pae] is complex, indeed, for it encompasses all the major ritual genres of traditional Māori society – warfare, intergroup hospitality and magic – but it is orderly, and the use of metaphor is systematic. It is this area that lends most conviction to a model based on intersecting opposites, because in the threshold zone the preoccupation is with balance, expressed in terms *utu* 'return, price, response, reply', *ea* 'be requited, be paid, be performed (rite), come up (crop)', and *rite* 'like, balanced, by equivalent, performed, completed'. (p. 16)

Salmond shows how this model of the Māori cosmos follows regular patterns, yet is complex enough to accommodate a wide range of concepts found in te reo Māori, and to apply across various domains of te ao Māori. This model of the Māori world as oriented by dynamic structuring binaries means that Māori ideas are inherently concerned with boundaries, liminal zones and movement between opposites: right action moves in the direction of life and light; wrong action moves towards the opposite.

This model of the Māori world makes sense of Indigenous Māori concepts that have no adequate English equivalent, since they do not fit within Western frameworks of knowledge. For example, the important Māori word 'mana' is usually translated as 'prestige' or 'power' but even in combination, these kinds of concepts fall short of its meaning, or more precisely, range of meanings, in the Māori world. In the dipolar Māori cosmos, mana exists in the ability to keep balanced or maintain utu; to stay in favour with the gods that personify the primal forces of the universe. The Māori world is profoundly metaphoric: in te reo Māori almost every lexical word can be used at many levels – literal, metaphorical and philosophical. Salmond's study, drawing on a wide range of concepts from early written sources, demonstrates how the language, te reo Māori, encapsulates ideas about the world, te ao Māori.

Salmond tested the 'explanatory value of the model' by reconsidering the 'hitherto unexplained and apparently eccentric ritual of biting the latrine beam' (p. 25). Her analysis showed that the horizontal latrine beam, referred to as a 'paepae' or a literal pae, was also a physical metaphor for the spiritual pae, this liminal zone called life that humans inhabit in between the oppositional cosmic forces. Thus, the traditional village latrine area was strongly associated with spiritual forces and atua (gods): the area in front of the beam was designated as tapu and the area behind the beam as noa. 'An informant called Tutaka says of the paepae: koinei te kai patu i te tangata, koinei te kai whakaora i te tangata "it is the killer of man, it is the curer of man"' (p. 25). Spiritual imbalance or imminent danger could be thwarted by certain rituals involving the latrine:

> The priest instructs him to bite the latrine beam, the head of the god, the seat of awesome power, to bite heaven and earth, above and below – in other words, to conquer orientational opposites and the threshold (paepae) that mediates them by the act of eating. (Salmond, 1978, p, 25)

This sense of binary pairs of opposite concepts is found in other examples from te reo Māori in addition to those explored in Salmond (1978). Another form is those Māori words that have two 'opposite' meanings. For example, 'ako' can mean either 'to teach' or 'to learn' depending on how it is used in a sentence. Ako has become widely used in education professional discourse, where the distorted idea has been promulgated that ako means both teach and learn, at the same time and without being able to be distinguished. In this way a 'Māori' concept has been used to further diminish the professional space available to the teacher in which to practice. Ako is therefore an example of malevolent education policy, in which an Indigenous word is taken up and distorted in policy in a way that disproportionately harms Māori children. Such is Māori reality in te ao hurihuri, to which discussion now turns.

Contemporary Māori reality

In Māori reality the Māori world is represented in and by te reo Māori, the Māori language. In other words, te reo Māori is both metaphor and metonym in relation to te ao Māori. Today it is hardly possible to inhabit a totally reo Māori universe, so the Māori linguistic world has a binary nature captured in the concept of bilingualism, which has been part of Māori experience since contact: a point of difference between Māori and Pākehā that has been overlooked in most non-Māori accounts. From a Māori perspective, te reo Pākehā (the English language) represents the wider world, and te reo Māori represents te ao Māori. For these reasons, bilingualism is central to biculturalism, another point that is frequently misunderstood – by Pākehā and also by some Māori commentators. What is called 'bicultural' in Aotearoa New Zealand is usually more accurately described as 'bi-ethnic' (preferable to 'bi-racial' – which was formerly used but fell out of favour several decades ago). Biculturalism is an important element of Māori ideas about the world, discussed in this and the following sections.

The contemporary Māori world therefore has a dual nature, echoing the dipolar nature of the traditional Indigenous Māori cosmos, discussed in the previous section. Like the Janus-face, one side looks to the past 'before the arrival of the Pākehā', which is still a frequently heard phrase in everyday Māori dialogue; the other side looks towards navigating the challenges of life in the twenty-first century. The contemporary Māori world is a symbolic world that resides in using te reo Māori, undertaking Māori practices, and the shared experience of being Māori. In reality the symbolic and physical worlds are inevitably entwined in the contemporary re-seeding of Indigenous practices, for example, moko kauae (chin tattoo) for women.

Contemporary situations like these invariably give rise to the question of authenticity, a notion that can be explored to help further unpack the full meanings (or at least our working meanings) of terms such as culture, knowledge and identity. At one extreme is the view that only pre-European artefacts, practices and technologies can be considered 'authentic' or 'real' Māori culture. Such views were strongly articulated (among Pākehā) in earlier phases of colonial history, when Pākehā were motivated to announce the end of the Māori world. These views are part of the fabric of 'everyday life' in Aotearoa New Zealand today, as te ao Māori has retreated into the background over time. In contrast, contemporary understandings of culture recognise that innovation is part of culture, and that replacing everyday technologies and surface features does not turn one culture into another, since these are not what are essential about a culture. One hears stories from non-Māori, often immigrants including British New Zealanders, who have experienced a revelation on their first experience of going to a marae, especially for a tangi (Māori funeral) and finding a 'world' they never knew existed: coming face to face with te ao Māori.

In the case of moko kauae, I can comment from recent personal experience. Moko artists today use the latest tattoo guns, as well as latex gloves and all the rest of it, but for me the experience of receiving a moko kauae in a day-long event (hui) held at the marae among my people was very special, authentic and completely unlike going to a tattoo shop. From the pōwhiri (formal welcome ceremony) in the morning to the shared feast as the sun was setting – one's first meal with a moko, together in a small hall with the other women who received their moko that day, along with families and supporters. A more jubilant contemporary example of te ao Māori would be difficult to find.

In the uncertain twenty-first century, Māori reality bears the brunt of economic restructuring and the rapid increase in statistical inequality. Māori families are under pressure like never before to help each other cope with the ongoing dismantling of the social welfare system and the rapid growth of economic inequality in what has formerly been a wealthy and egalitarian society. Attitudes in Aotearoa New Zealand are influenced by overseas trends, which have recently hardened markedly with the rise of the global right, as reflected in the Trump presidency. Pākehā have long felt secure in their domination over Māori. History becomes a thing of the past as social amnesia, that old ally of colonial powers, is further encouraged by the presentism that suffuses neoliberal thinking, resulting in the 'blame-the-victim' mentality. Thus in the public media, Māori get blamed for their own increasing statistical impoverishment, with ongoing stereotyping as lazy dole-bludgers, updating the generally racist ways in which media have presented Māori throughout history (Moewaka-Barnes, Borell, Taiapa, Rankine, & McCreanor, 2012).

A Māori viewpoint on things is quite the opposite: in comparison with Western culture, Māori thinking is oriented to the past. In te reo Māori the phrase 'i mua' means 'before' in both senses: past time and in front of us. The paired phrase is 'i muri' which means both after in time and behind us. In Māori thinking, the past is before us because we can see it; we walk backwards into the future since we cannot look and see what it will bring. This orientation to the world encourages us to reflect on and learn from the past. The time is still almost within living memory when tribal authorities directed Māori lives. I have a friend whose mother told him family stories passed down from being at the 1814 event in the Bay of Islands when Samuel Marsden addressed a gathering of local iwi on Christmas Day. This event is known in national archives and to the Anglican church as the 'first sermon' – though if the audience cannot understand English, can a sermon be said to have been preached? (Jones, 2005). My friend's mother said the people had no idea what Marsden was talking about, but were struck by the sadness with which he spoke.

My aunt told me about the time when her mother, my grandmother Tangiaranui, left my patriarch of a grandfather and moved to Auckland, where my aunt and other members of the younger generation were living, in the early modern New Zealand economy of the interwar period. My aunt was working as a domestic servant for a rich Pākehā family living on Tamaki Drive. She recalled the kaumātua (male elder) from their small rural community up north coming to Auckland after some weeks had passed, and telling her mother 'Enough is enough' upon which her mother went straight away to get her bag ready for the trip home, in case she lost the opportunity to gather her things.

The way 'kaumātua' are spoken about today, especially in non-Māori domains such as schools, gestures towards these Indigenous traditions, but all too easily descends into caricature. The growing practice of holding Māori welcome ceremonies at occasions such as conferences can be an ambivalent performance of culture that often means more to non-Māori participants than to Māori, who understand the subtle differences between 'corporate Māori' and 'culturally Māori' occasions (Stewart, Tamatea, & Mika, 2015). The binary Māori world of today is inevitably an ambivalent, uncomfortable space to inhabit. The longstanding lack of understanding and respect shown towards Māori culture and history in public institutions has become part of, if not characteristic of, Māori experience in te ao hurihuri. My mother wrote a literary essay about the famous traditional waiata (song) *E pā tō hau* in which she succinctly expressed this past-oriented dual nature of Māori experience:

> To the Māori psyche, growing up in the contemporary world has a special bitterness: it brings the realisation that the people are no longer in control, but are constantly forced to operate within systems that

originated outside Māori tradition. The land, Papatūānuku, remains, but her face is in many places transformed beyond recognition. Nostalgia for the past offers temporary escape and refreshment, where the paradisal dream of unfettered self-fulfilment can be experienced. The days gone by cannot be brought back; it is the here and now with which we must deal. The Pākehā is here to stay and his blood runs in our veins. All those tragic words conveying loss, shrinkage and alienation express the shock of the modern world. Yet the dream lives on, remade every time we mourn it. (Menzies, 1993, p. 57)

Māori are often exhorted to forget the past and look to the future, which is about as futile as telling Māori that they are not 'real' Māori. Outspoken critic of Māori education Elizabeth Rata accuses other scholars of exaggerating the differences between Māori and Pākehā for ideological reasons (Rata, 2012). But why should people forget their own history? And how can Māori 'get over' what happened to their people when it has never been publicly admitted; indeed, when Pākehā myths have been deliberately inculcated to conceal it? The right to self-identify ethnicity is a basic bastion of democracy in Aotearoa New Zealand: to remove this right would be politically impossible (at the time of writing). On the other hand, Māori accept that the Pākehā world is here to stay and must be dealt with. I therefore reason that Māori should embrace biculturalism, on our terms, as the logical alternative to the dominant monoculturalism. The two sections below further explore contemporary Māori experience of cultural difference, and the meaning of biculturalism on Māori terms.

Living in two worlds

All humans live in one physical world, on this one planet: we are all subject to the same natural and social forces that determine the context in which we live our lives (Lugones, 1987). In contemporary Aotearoa New Zealand, 'living in two worlds' means living in different segments of society – a brute economic fact reflecting the statistical division of wealth along ethnic lines. The feeling of living in two worlds is also a matter of living with two worldviews: living across the threshold between te ao Māori and te ao Pākehā. The concept of 'worldview' is understood as a personal–cultural ontological, epistemological and ethical paradigm. The human world is in part a symbolic world, in which our direct experience of the world is mediated through language and the cultural narratives with which we identify. Te ao Māori is partly a symbolic world that exists in te reo Māori, in Māori histories, and as represented in books and other written material and imagery, including the metaphors and stories contained in this book.

Te ao Māori has been a topic of great interest to scholars and students in a wide range of fields of inquiry since first contact with te ao Pākehā. Māori are one of the most heavily researched of all the different peoples of the world (L. T. Smith, 2012). Books on all kinds of Māori topics have been and continue to be published; there is also a healthy academic literature that intersects with te ao Māori. The 'Māori' factor has a holographic nature in the sense that it can be related to almost any topic. Put another way, te ao Māori acts like a lens or optical filter through which we view the world around us. My interest for some time has been in better understanding and describing the undeniable difference of the Māori worldview, expressed as 'living in two worlds', which is routinely experienced by Māori people, including myself, though seemingly invisible to the sciences, and accordingly denied by many non-Māori scholars and commentators.

An oppositional academic debate concerning the claims of Indigenous knowledge has been underway for at least fifty years, taking several forms in various fields over time. For example, the classical anthropological debate about 'rationality' posited science against Indigenous knowledge, in efforts to clarify what science actually is, and how it works (Wilson, 1970). Second, the ongoing 'science wars' centre on the 'two cultures' in the academy, represented by the question of the status of 'social science' as science (Sokal, 1996a, b). Third, in work influential on education theory, Jerome Bruner (1986) proposed two basic modes of thought: 'narrative' and 'logico-scientific'.

There are many variations of the binary model of thinking, and in many cases, such as Bruner's theory, logic is assigned to one side of the binary, thereby leaving it out of the other. But anthropology suggests logical coherence is characteristic of all cultural knowledge bases, Western and non-Western (e.g. Māori, see Salmond, 1985). So, it makes little sense to assign logic to 'scientific' thought, since narrative power also depends upon logical coherence. But although Eurocentrism has been expelled from the academy, the association of science with modern Western culture as 'proof' that Euro-Americans are more 'advanced' than 'primitive races' remains a powerful 'subterranean' message in social discourse, retaining influence even within academia (Wetherell & Potter, 1992). This reference to a classic study of racialised discourse in Aotearoa New Zealand, while dated, is still applicable today.

The two modes of thought are better known today as 'left brain' and 'right brain' thinking (Lamb, 2004). As part of the common heritage of all human beings, the left-brain/right-brain model of thinking helps in seeking to avoid the usual Eurocentric influences. Cognitive science and brain medicine have established that left-brain thinking is typically analytical in nature, while right-brain thinking is holistic. These two modes of thought are reflected in two basic modes of language, which I will call 'measurement' and 'metaphor'. This view sees logic as inherent in both modes of thinking and therefore in both modes of language operation. To omit logic from the criteria for making distinctions between the two basic modes of thought (metaphor and measurement each employing logic in their own way) eases the longstanding debates about rationality, epistemological diversity and incommensurability (Siegel, 2006).

Modern English and science have co-evolved so that today the English language reflects the influence of the modernist, deterministic philosophy of science (Halliday, 2004). Science discourse requires that words and sentences have precise and unambiguous meanings. Although rich, messy stories from the history of science are preserved within science words, such as the names of the elements, in its operation science language is profoundly non-metaphorical: nouns, verbs and adjectives have stable, precisely defined meanings; and statements are intended to be understood literally, not metaphorically. Scientific English sacrifices richness of meaning in favour of precision: words and statements have single-layered meanings (not to be confused with the idea of simple versus complex meanings).

Speakers of Māori will recognise that the above descriptions of scientific English are foreign, if not antithetical to the workings of te reo Māori. In te reo Māori, even very small words carry many levels and nuances of meaning, within an overall worldview built from the large tropes, narratives and metaphors of traditional Māori culture. Not only are Māori words and phrases multileveled in meaning, but a great deal of the meaning of Māori words and statements rests in exactly how they are said by the speaker. Thus, oratory is far more important in Māori culture than in modern Western culture. Sacrificing precision for richness of meaning is associated with this performative aspect of language in te reo Māori that is absent from modern scientific English.

Sydney Lamb (2004) maps 'left brain' and 'right brain' thinking onto 'philosophical differences' he terms 'splitter thinking' (associated with absolutism, universalism and reductionism) and 'lumper thinking' (associated with relativism and holism), respectively. Perhaps, then, traditional Māori language reflects a cultural worldview operating as much by holistic right-brain thinking as by the analytical left-brain mode. Modern English is influenced by the scientific genre, reflecting the dominance of measurement-oriented left-brain thinking, using precise, stable, literal meanings, which can be represented in written form without loss of semantic content. In te reo Māori, however, lexical words play a far lesser role in carrying meaning, which has more to do with how lexical words are arranged between many other small words. Over and above the words themselves, much of the meaning of a Māori utterance rests in the pacing and emphasis of each word, along with facial expression, gesture and the use of other language devices, such as repetition, or extra non-lexical words added in for emphasis. Might not the concept of cultural worldview and the claims about epistemological diversity be explainable in terms of (among other things) a relative balance between these two modes of measurement (left brain) and metaphor (right brain) language and thinking?

The characteristics of left-brain thinking have invalidly come to be identified with the nature of science, in a way that supports certain forms of scientism or ideological distortions of science, including the claims made by neoliberal economics to include 'scientific' approaches to social policy (P. Roberts & Peters, 2008). The overbalance of 'measurement' in favour of 'metaphor' modes of thinking and language seems characteristic of neoliberal discourse – lots of information but no wisdom, a checklist approach that misses the 'bigger picture'. The discourses, worldviews and epistemologies associated with Indigenous cultural cosmologies, and the languages in which they are expressed, such as te reo and te ao Māori, may differ most importantly from those of modern Western science and culture in terms of relative balance between these two great psychological modes of operation, each related in extremely complex ways with its own specialist hemisphere of the human brain organ. (Of course, this proposal is not to be understood as returning to any sort of outmoded notion of biological differences related to 'intelligence' between ethnic groups.) To conceptualise different forms of thinking in relation to philosophy and language in this way supports the assertion of a coherent concept of epistemological difference between Māori knowledge and Pākehā knowledge, while clearly showing a continuity between the two. This model also explains why the differences between Māori and Pākehā worldviews (te ao Māori me te ao Pākehā) cannot be captured at the level of individual words, but require exposition at the level of metaphor, narrative or discourse.

The link between languages and worldviews is a central concept in the larger knowledge debates referred to above (Cooper & Spolsky, 1991). The Sapir-Whorf hypothesis (Whorf, 1956) is one well-known iteration of this idea that retains its attraction, despite failing in its strong form to be demonstrated by empirical studies, and hence losing out to the concept of 'universal grammar' in the dominant paradigms of linguistics (Schlesinger, 1991). This snippet from intellectual history seems to exemplify the larger problem of Western knowledge that blinds itself to such undeniable truth as the phenomenon of cultural worldview, captured in language. The difference between Western and Indigenous languages is reflected in divergent worldviews or concepts about reality, and this difference has been described as a source of important cognitive resources for humanity (Fishman, 1982).

The significance of Māori philosophy is based on this notion of epistemological diversity as a valuable cognitive resource. These benefits of language diversity, therefore, rest on te reo Māori retaining its traditional forms and being 'different' from English. This recognition of the importance of difference counters the drive to modernise and standardise te reo Māori, which involves a process of 'fixing' the meanings of traditional Māori words aligned with Pākehā concepts (Mika, 2012) in which the 'richness of imprecision' is lost, and with it, the value of te reo Māori as a linguistic articulation of te ao Māori. This would be a tragic loss of cultural heritage for Māori people, a national loss to Aotearoa New Zealand, and a reduction in the cognitive resources available to humanity that would also entail a loss for all human beings – just as we all lose when any Indigenous language dies (Crystal, 2000).

Biculturalism and the hyphen

Māori philosophy is a useful lens for conceptual discussion of binaries and boundaries, which are important on account of their prominence in both the traditional and contemporary Māori worlds. Various terms have been used over the years to refer to the interface between cultures, including biculturalism, cross-culturalism and, more recently, interculturalism (Besley & Peters, 2012). I adopt the term 'intercultural hyphen' on the view that all these terms operate more-or-less synonymously, while remaining open to interpretation. Inherent in the position from which I write is the recognition that the essence of te ao Māori resides in Māori thinking and thought, which I refer to as 'Māori philosophy'. To describe Māori philosophy is also to describe Māori ideas about reality and the world.

Living in the contemporary Māori world, as argued above, means negotiating across the boundaries between te ao Māori and the outside world. Māori have been 'bicultural' since the early days of British incursion into Aotearoa, which gives Māori a formidable advantage in navigating these boundaries. The increased national awareness in recent decades of a history of unfair policies for Māori has resulted in sympathetic Pākehā seeing 'biculturalism' as the answer – but such Pākehā notions of biculturalism do not usually account for Māori perspectives. In response, many Māori have rejected 'biculturalism' as 'not Māori enough' and argue for 'Kaupapa Māori' instead. But at the same time, it is recognised that being Māori today means constant navigation between these two worlds, or worldviews, since the Indigenous person is inevitably aware of ethnic boundaries at many levels. A rebooted radical Māori form of biculturalism, based on critical Māori accounts of history and philosophy, works as a critical or Kaupapa Māori approach to biculturalism, which, I would suggest, is in Māori interests to promulgate and develop.

The intercultural hyphen is useful as a model for the boundary between Māori and Pākehā cultures that accommodates Kaupapa Māori or critical Māori perspectives. The intercultural hyphen is a metaphor or model for the boundary implied within the concept of ethnicity, which comes into being through contact between different cultural groups (Eriksen, 2002). In this sense, ethnicity exists only in relationship, and has no independent existence: it is not a hard-and-fast 'thing' or category. This view of ethnicity makes the hyphen a useful model of biculturalism, which is language based, the hyphen being a punctuation mark, and suitable as a model of the Māori-Pākehā relationship, which is central in Aotearoa New Zealand (Hoskins, 2012). The term 'Māori-Pākehā' is a specific or localised example of the intercultural hyphen, while 'Indigenous-settler' refers to this generic or global type of sociohistorical relationship, in which both terms

'Indigenous' and 'settler' act as place holders for the actual peoples involved in the specific intercultural relationship in each context.

The Māori-Pākehā hyphen is explored in the influential handbook chapter by Alison Jones and Kuni Jenkins, titled *Rethinking Collaboration: Working the Indigene-Coloniser Hyphen* (Jones & Jenkins, 2008) Jones argues for the value of the hyphen as a symbol of the relationship and link between Māori and Pākehā that does not necessarily obliterate either identity. She describes her collaboration with Jenkins, to research the early history of Māori education in Northland from 1816 onwards, as 'working the hyphen' – an example she uses to show the potential benefits of this approach. Jones and Jenkins adapt the metaphor of 'working the hyphen' from Michelle Fine's (1994) examination of how social science has contributed to creating cultural Others for Western purposes. Using the hyphen model, Jones and Jenkins demonstrate the paradoxical, bipolar or two-faced nature of the intercultural space, summing up Pākehā responses to the encounter with indigeneity as cultural difference as follows:

A marker of the relationship between two generalized groups, the hyphen has been erased, softened, denied, consumed, expanded, homogenized, and romanticized. The discursive hyphen has stood in for an unbridgeable chasm between the civilized and the uncivilized; it has marked a romantic difference between the innocent noble savage and corrupt Western man; it has held the gap between the indigenous subjects of study and their objective White observers. (Jones & Jenkins, 2008, p. 473)

Kaupapa Māori theory itself can be seen as a theory of biculturalism in that it is an assertion of Māori resistance to the deleterious effects of Pākehā domination. Kaupapa Māori, in other words, overturns the colonial binary in which Pākehā dominate and Māori are oppressed. In this sense, the two-word term 'Kaupapa Māori' acts as an adjectival phrase meaning the opposite of 'Eurocentric'. But there are two ways to understand what 'the opposite of Eurocentric' refers to: either as an innocent (or uncritical) interpretation or as a critical one. For strategic purposes, Kaupapa Māori has promoted a reified view of Māori culture as more homogeneous and less fragmentary than it really is (Hoskins, 2012). The innocent version of Kaupapa Māori is taken in by the strategy, overlooking the fact that a strategy is 'a means to a particular end within a prevailing logic that we more fundamentally reject' (p. 87). For Māori,

> [t]he indigenous inversion or reversal of positions within the binary to 'the inherently good Māori' and 'inherently bad coloniser', while perhaps challenging persistent colonial assumptions, is ultimately an unsustainable position – one without a future. (Hoskins, 2012, p. 86)

The argument here is that both Māori and Pākehā can easily confuse the ideological with the material levels of this hyphen – this boundary between Māori and Pākehā worldviews and identities. For Māori, this confusion no doubt relates to the doubled nature of Māori identity, on top of the oppressive weight of history and its concomitant subordination within the dominant 'European' culture. Pākehā confusion, on the other hand, reflects strenuous disengagement from Māori (Bell, 2014), including discontinuous views of history and the associated Pākehā inability to 'hear' Māori voices (Jones & Jenkins, 2008).

The reason why the innocent version of Kaupapa Māori described above has no future is because it is based on a fictional version of Māori subjectivity: one, moreover, that originates in a Pākehā colonising binary. Innocent versions of Kaupapa Māori include Māori versions of hyphen-denial and rejection of biculturalism. Innocent versions of Kaupapa Māori include 'purist' aspirations that reject all things Pākehā – what is sometimes called wanting to live in a 'Māori bubble'. This 'Māori-only' approach inexorably involves discontinuous views of history, just as noted above for Pākehā. Māori do not have to be 'the same' as Pākehā in order to enjoy all the fruits of human knowledge, according to democratic values of social justice. An example of this sort of problem is when Māori university 'students evoke Kaupapa Māori research methodologies and declare that they are, therefore, only reading scholarly work by Māori writers' (Hoskins, 2012, p. 88).

Drawing on work by Alice Punga-Somerville, Hoskins uses terms such as 'diminishing rather than space-opening', 'closed', 'orthodoxy' and 'self-referential' to describe forms of uncritical Kaupapa Māori thinking (pp. 88–89).

Conversely, the critical version of Kaupapa Māori is cognisant of the limits of strategy, and the difference between strategy and reality. Kaupapa Māori theory includes or allows space for the intercultural hyphen, which brings into play the second, more critical meaning of the phrase 'the opposite of Eurocentric'. In this sense, it means engaging 'as Māori' with te ao Māori me te ao hurihuri. This also suggests that the meaning of 'Kaupapa Māori' can be equated with the hybrid word 'Māori-centric'. This perspective reveals 'Māori-only' approaches in the name of Kaupapa Māori as limiting and unhelpful, ultimately, to Māori interests. Kaupapa Māori scholarship that ignores the hyphen remains mired within the binary: innocent and at risk of being domesticated (Smith, 2012).

Questions for discussion or research

- Find out about other cultural traditions concerning the origins of the world, humans and knowledge, and assess how these are similar or dissimilar to the Māori accounts summarised in this chapter.
- Does the translation of philosophical concepts from Indigenous languages into English necessarily distort the Indigenous concepts, and if so, why? Suggest strategies for working with such distortions.

Māori knowledge

While Māori people and their lands were being colonised under Victorian imperialism, Māori people and their language and knowledge were also simultaneously becoming a legitimate object of European study in the emerging disciplines of the modern academy, particularly those of anthropology, linguistics and sociology. At the same time, Māori knowledge, as part of Indigenous knowledge more generally, marks the boundary that defines the canons of science and philosophy (referred to below as 'Western knowledge' while recalling the caveats about this term as discussed in Chapter 1 above, pages 3–5). Any item or aspect of Indigenous knowledge found useful by science is stripped away from its cultural context and incorporated into the Western canon in a process of epistemic colonisation, while Indigenous knowledge itself, in its holistic entirety, integrated with culture and language, remains excluded by definition. So Indigenous (or Māori) knowledge forms part of the boundary between science, equated with 'real knowledge', on the one hand, and religion, folklore, superstition or 'not-knowledge', on the other hand. This boundary produces a fundamental paradox in the popular idea of 'reconciling' science and Māori knowledge as 'Māori science' – a phrase most scientists would consider a basic contradiction in terms.

Māori knowledge does not conform to the disciplines and fields of Western knowledge, which immediately throws up obstacles for any attempt to include Māori knowledge in domains such as education that are founded on Western knowledge traditions. Evidence from te reo Māori shows that Māori ideas about thinking were associated with the activity of the stomach and entrails. The word 'hinengaro' that is standard today for 'mind' or 'intellect' was in traditional language also a word for the spleen or stomach, which was considered the 'seat of the thoughts and emotions' (Williams, 1971). Such examples show how in Māori ideas the mind was regarded more like a 'body-mind' as against the scientific view of the brain organ being the physical location of the mind. This is typical of the trend in Māori knowledge towards the holistic, and in Western knowledge towards the compartmentalised. Examples such as this, where the Māori version of an idea is holistic while the Western is atomised, can be found in every direction of inquiry in Māori philosophy.

Māori ideas about knowledge

Māori ideas about knowledge derive from Māori understandings of the world and of inter-relationships between humankind and the world. Māori ideas about knowledge are carried in the narratives and oral texts of Māori traditions, which underwrite social relationships and cultural practices. Māori knowledge is expressed in and through Māori language: Māori philosophy, language, identity and culture form one integrated whole, and any attempt to describe and analyse one part of this complex in isolation from the whole must be accepted as only partial. The categories of Western knowledge as reflected in the academic disciplines, the English language, and the systems of societal expertise and authority, are inimical to the perception and characterisation of Māori knowledge on its own terms. Thus, not only individual Māori concepts but also the holistic structure of Māori philosophy itself is unable adequately to be described within English-language categories. Delineations of Māori knowledge in English (including this one) are unsatisfactory in (at least) two ways: they tend towards oversimplification, often producing caricatures or cartoon versions of Māori knowledge, and they gesture towards an uncrossable abyss or boundary, beyond which lies an unknowable Māori reality that can never be attained. This being accepted, it is still worth trying to make some comments about Māori philosophy of knowledge, from a Māori researcher perspective.

The cosmogenic narratives of the primordial familial Māori gods as outlined above in the previous chapter were recorded as primary anthropological data, in the Eurocentric milieu of Victorian science that underwrote the colonisation of Aotearoa and other lands distant from England and Europe. More local oral texts such as Te Whare Tapu o Ngāpuhi have also passed into the public domain insofar as they can be looked up online. These disclaimers reassure the Indigenous author, such as myself: they are a way of demonstrating that I am not revealing private or sacred knowledge in this book. It must be conceded that in order to be able to consider the possibility of knowledge being private or sacred, one has arguably already passed beyond the point where it matters one way or the other. In the modern way of thinking the idea of 'intellectual property' as sacred or private knowledge has been overtaken by a concept of 'commercial sensitivity' – knowledge that provides a competitive advantage, equated with monetary profit and competitive advantage, and always underpinned by the protection of military power.

A memorable story about Māori understandings of powerful knowledge is attributed to Māori Marsden, an elder from the far north who I met several times in the last decade of his life before he died in 1993.[1] This vignette is included in Te Ahukaramū Charles Royal's edited book of Marsden's talks and writings, *The Woven Universe*. Marsden was an ordained minister in the Anglican church, a tohunga trained in traditional Māori knowledge and a university-educated scholar. Marsden recounts a conversation he held with the Ngāpuhi elders at the final set of traditional wānanga (expert schools), convened after the end of the Second World War. All dialogue at such events was conducted in te reo. One of the elders asked Marsden to explain the difference between an explosive bomb and an atomic bomb, since they were aware that the latter had brought the war to an end, so Marsden expressed the phenomenon of nuclear fission using the traditional word 'hihiri' meaning 'pure energy'. Marsden continues:

> [The elder] then exclaimed 'Do you mean to tell me that the Pākehā scientists (tohunga Pākehā) have managed to rend the fabric (kahu) of the universe?' I said 'Yes' 'I suppose they shared their knowledge with the tūtūā (politicians)?' 'Yes' 'But do they know how to sew (tuitui) it back together again?' 'No!' 'That's the trouble with sharing such "tapu" knowledge. Tūtūā will always abuse it.' (Royal, 2003, p. 57)

This story brilliantly showcases the use of Māori philosophical frameworks, invoking the metaphor of the heavens as the cloak of Ranginui, and their ability to produce truth and wisdom without the need for scientific vocabulary, theory or its underpinning Western philosophical commitments.

In introducing this book of Marsden's writings, Royal (2003) comments on 'the way we Māori feel today about our Māoritanga. There is this sense that the version of Māoritanga that we possess and exhibit today is not quite the real thing, that it is somehow inferior' (p. x). Royal records his acute sense of loss after Marsden died, and how this feeling of disconnection was later ameliorated by his work of reading and arranging Marsden's extensive collection of manuscripts, now held in the Auckland City Library. Royal concludes that Marsden 'has bequeathed to us a complex and sophisticated model of a Māoritanga that is appropriate for us today' (p. x). With this in mind, the next section leans on Marsden's accounts, as recorded in this valuable resource book.

The baskets of knowledge – ngā kete o te wānanga

Tāne seemed to be the busiest of the atua (deities). Having separated his parents by pushing away his father to allow light to enter the world, then clothing and adorning his newly exposed parents, Tāne in his guise as Tāne-nui-a-Rangi ascended to the highest heavens and returned with three pūtea (container or store of valuables, now used mainly for funds) or kete (baskets) of knowledge for humankind, known as 'ngā kete e toru o te wānanga' or the three baskets of knowledge, which Marsden also describes as 'ao' or worlds (Royal, 2003, pp. 60–2). These kete were, firstly, te kete tuauri, often glossed as the basket of sacred knowledge, including karakia. Marsden describes this kete as the 'real world' behind the world of sensory perception (equivalent, perhaps, to the 'worlds' described by the basic sciences of chemistry and physics). The second kete is te kete aronui, which is knowledge of the natural world around us: reality as apprehended by the senses. Third is te kete tuatea, or tuaātea according to Marsden, who describes it as the world beyond space and time, the transcendent realm of the gods.

The 'three baskets of knowledge' is an example of a fragment of Māori philosophy that has been appropriated countless times in many forms of knowledge activity, such as in schools, libraries or websites, to the point that it has become a 'Kiwi metaphor' for knowledge. There are many versions on record of these traditions, details of which are inconsistent and sometimes contradictory. In some accounts, one kete contains esoteric knowledge such as magic and incantations, while another contains practical knowledge such as carving and agriculture. Some traditions assign alternative sets of names for the kete, and some iwi traditions attribute the feat of obtaining the kete to Tāwhaki rather than Tāne. Nonetheless, the central idea of three distinct funds of knowledge, obtained from unearthly realms and gifted to humanity by an ancestor deity, is common to all iwi groups.

Marsden adds that Tāne also brought back two stones of knowledge, a detail omitted from most popularised accounts of Māori narratives

of knowledge. Kōhatu (stones) play an important role in traditional
Māori ideas about knowledge, as physical repositories for metaphysical
energies/entities of knowledge and power. It seems the density of
stone was regarded as being capable of 'holding' spiritual energy.[2] Not
only were stone tools used in technologies that sustained life, such
as gardening and weaving, but stone objects called 'atua' or 'mauri'
were used as talismans to secure the integrity and life force of a place
or activity, such as a garden. In the winter months, during the non-
growing season, was the time of year when wānanga (teaching and
learning sessions) were held. Sitting in the pitch dark of a winter's night,
the pupils were said to hold stones in their mouths, to help them learn
and memorise the content of the wānanga.

Central concepts in Māori philosophy

This section presents brief explanations of some central terms related
to Māori ideas about knowledge and thinking. Due to the differences
between traditional Māori and modern scientific worldviews, many
Māori words do not have exact English equivalents, therefore requiring
paragraph explanations, rather than single words or short phrases. This
difficulty with translation is even more acute for the large Indigenous
philosophical concepts included below. The list approach for explaining
Māori concepts has precedent, especially the useful reference book
Tikanga Whakaaro: Key Concepts in Māori Culture (Barlow, 1991), and
provides a convenient way of organising the material. But caution must
be exercised in working with this format, since these Māori concepts
do not stand alone: they are inter-related within an overall framework
of Māori understanding of reality that derives from the cosmogenic
narratives described in the previous chapter. An alphabetical list of
Māori concepts subjects them to a foreign symbolic order, with its
own power. Rather, key Māori concepts are explained below, grouped
and sequenced in ways that make sense in terms of the overall Māori
worldview.

The first list showcases some key philosophical Māori concepts and values; the second part explains a few Māori words related to knowledge. Many of these Māori words and concepts have become common in New Zealand English, but often with truncated or distorted meanings. This section pays attention to this process of distortion by translation, with the aim to reconcile meanings with a Māori-centric perspective, showcasing how each concept works within an integrated overall Māori worldview.

Central Māori concepts and values

Whakapapa

Whakapapa is the central concept in Māori culture and an organising principle in Māori philosophy. The meaning of whakapapa is approximated by the word 'genealogy', but its full range of meanings extends far beyond the everyday understanding of genealogy as 'family tree'. The word whakapapa translates as something like 'layer-upon-layer' – made up of the causative prefix 'whaka-' and the stem word 'papa' with a literal meaning of ground or layer, and which calls to Papatūānuku at every utterance (Mika, 2017) – hence giving the meaning of 'to make layers' or something like 'generative' (Barlow, 1991).

Whakapapa is a master concept of the Māori worldview and key to understanding Indigenous Māori views of the natural and social worlds, and guiding right ethical relationships between people, and between humans and other living and non-living things. The nature narratives of the Māori creation story are a model for how the concept of whakapapa works for organising arrays of complex information. In traditional Māori society, whakapapa knowledge was of both economic and social value (Firth, 1972) in many ways: as a basis for the individual's identity, rights, residence, status, occupation and possible life partners and companions. Whakapapa is rather like each person being a knot within a large and ever-expanding metaphorical fishing net of connections, in contrast with the modern economistic view of individuals as more like single unbonded atoms of an inert gas, freely moving at random within their physical limits.

Whakapapa is visually represented in Māori iconography by the double helix spiral motif seen in elaborate carved works such as the prow of a large ceremonial waka (canoe) or carved posts in the whare (houses). There are two spiral forms in Māori art and hence in Māori thought: first the common koru, or simple spiral, inspired by the furled baby fern frond, signalling growth of all kinds; and secondly the takarangi or double helix spiral, which represents whakapapa and also time, and therefore space-time, since the word 'wā' was originally used for both, suggesting space and time in the Māori worldview are connected. Each notch in the carved double spiral pattern stands for a generation, which is one way in which such carved items were used as graphical heuristics for teaching and learning whakapapa. It is also a way of reckoning long periods of time, based upon the inexact unit of a generation. The words 'tātai' and 'whakaheke' have similar meanings as whakapapa, but refer to specific descent lines, not necessarily implying all the larger levels of meaning of whakapapa.

Whakapapa in its full cultural meaning highlights the characteristic of Māori thought and discourse to prefer spiral structures, rather than the typical linear structure favoured by Western notions of knowledge, particularly in logic, mathematics and science. The spiral shape and the concept of whakapapa are metaphors for the great family of Rangi and Papa. In other words, Māori bodies of knowledge take the form of whakapapa and its accompanying stories. Whakapapa in a general sense is also a concept, a value and a 'way of thinking' (Barton, 1993, p. 59), 'both a noun and a verb' (McKinley, 2003, p. 21). 'Māori use of whakapapa and narrative creates a "metaphysical gestalt" or whole, integrated pattern, for the oral communication of knowledge' (Roberts et al., 2004, p. 1). In this way the single word 'whakapapa' acts like a one-word synopsis, metonym and hologram of a complete Indigenous worldview, comprising the cultural narratives that structure and keep in place all the related Māori concepts and values, including those described below.

The unusual double helix shape that represents whakapapa coincides with the shape of the DNA molecule, a rather remarkable convergence given that DNA is the literal manifestation of whakapapa in the sense of one's biological inheritance, and that which causes a person to resemble their forebears. In recent decades science has discovered that in their DNA, people literally carry their ancestors with them throughout life. This science fact echoes the ancient Māori belief that forms the basis of the rationale for the cultural practice in formal encounters of karanga (calling), which is addressed to the ancestors that a group of people in a tapu state carry with them at a spiritual level, as explained above in Chapter 3 (see page 32). Understanding whakapapa and space-time as both part of a spiral structure also enriches the concept of 'mataora' or 'living face' which refers to the power by which ancestors 'could collapse space-time to become co-present with their descendants' (Salmond, 1997, p. 32), a notion that makes more sense in a spiral, rather than linear or Western, concept of time.

Whakapapa as a spiral notion of space-time works together with the dipolar model of the Māori cosmos (see page 61) with its multiple intersecting 'pou', each holding apart one of the primal dichotomies, to structure both taiao (environment) and hinengaro (mind), in the process forming the 'pae' or liminal zones where actual moral discourse occurs. These elements combine to form a coherent value concept structure, reflected and represented in te reo Māori, through which mātauranga engages the phenomenological world. 'In other words, language is related to culture in both a metonymical and a metaphorical way' (Hastrup, 1982, p. 153). From this engagement arise the 'Māori values' (Patterson, 1992) that have been rehearsed in many published iterations over the years (Durie, 2005). In combination, these ideas provide a reasonably robust overall sense of how mātauranga differs from Western rationality, accounting for the way linguistic relativity (W1) is often experienced as a cognitive dissonance though contact with a non-Western language and culture such as Māori.

The homology between whakapapa and evolution suggests Māori philosophy is potentially useful in relation to cases of evolutionism, or misuses of evolutionary theory. Evolutionary debates are many and varied and include a range of extreme positions along the scientism-to-antiscience spectrum. Examples include 'creation science' at one pole, and 'selfish gene' theories at the other, both found in operation in the same social context of the contemporary United States. Evolutionary ideology or 'evolutionism' operates at both lay and academic levels in complex and covert ways to reinforce and safeguard the interests of the global elite (Gould, 1997; Herrnstein & Murray, 1996).

Whakapapa is the ethical basis of the celebrated Māori respect and love for nature that is consistent with the general characteristic of Indigenous peoples of living in harmony with nature. The 'whakapapa kōrero' (Smith, 2000) found in Māori sayings and nature narratives are rich parables, or teaching stories. To understand oneself as literally related to all the living and non-living elements of the natural world as common descendants of Rangi and Papa makes a coherent reason for taking care of nature, an ethos Māori Marsden defined as 'kaitiakitanga' (Royal, 2003, p. 67). From an academic perspective, John Patterson delineated the Māori ethos underwritten by whakapapa as an 'environmental virtue ethic' (Patterson, 2000, p. 46) consisting of some big ideas arising from the cosmogenic whakapapa narratives such as whanaungatanga (kinship) and kaitiakitanga, as well as 'personal qualities required to be good citizens of the natural world' (p. 45).

The Indigenous concept of whakapapa is the key point of difference between Māori philosophy and Western philosophy, each understood on their own terms, that causes theoretical incommensurability or disparity between them. The concept of the relationship between humans and the natural world in Māori philosophy is whakapapa, as the above paragraphs have established. The corresponding Western concept is referred to in the Bible as humans having 'dominion over' animals and nature. In his investigation of the essence of technology, Martin Heidegger described a fundamental attitude of 'enframing' in Western culture towards nature, in other words seeing the world around us only in terms of our own needs and wants, and regarding natural resources as 'standing reserves' to serve our interests: quantifiable raw materials to use up at will. These attitudes are built into language, such as the modern meanings of words such as 'resource' and 'interests' 'sustainability' and 'management' being tied to monetary profit in economistic thinking.

This opposing pair of concepts – whakapapa versus standing reserve – exemplifies what Lyotard calls the 'differend' since it is a central point of tension between Western (Pākehā or mainstream) thinking and Māori thinking, which results in countless specific disputes over land rights, resource management and so on, all around Aotearoa. But the law cannot account for this philosophical difference, since it does not and cannot 'think' whakapapa, so Western attitudes and frameworks of understanding invariably trump Māori (and environmentalist) arguments, ably supported by the weight of centuries of belief in the superiority of the European and the consequent rights of Pākehā interests to prevail over those of Māori. These beliefs are boosted each time Māori views or aspirations are scuttled by the courts or other authorities.

Whakapapa forms the theoretical framework of Māori knowledge, to which all other Māori concepts are attached, which is why it comes first in this section. The remaining list of selected concepts below is not exhaustive, but includes some key Māori concepts, focusing on how each one fits into the overall Māori worldview or philosophy, links to the central framework provided by the master concept of whakapapa, and helps build up an overall flexible guide for ethical Māori thinking and practice, across a wide range of activities.

Mana, tapu

Mana is approximated by power, authority or prestige, while tapu is equated to sacred, or set apart. Mana and tapu are two key philosophical Māori concepts, impossible to fully understand and hence prone to distortion, in the absence of an overall appreciation of the Indigenous

Māori worldview. These two words (or their cognates) are also found in related Pacific languages including of Hawai'i, Samoa, Tonga and Rarotonga. Tapu (in Tongan, tabu) was appropriated into English as 'taboo', a concept introduced to England by Captain James Cook, in an example of how such voyages in the Age of Discovery harvested cognitive resources, in addition to biological and other natural phenomena, for extending European systems of knowledge. Today, both tapu and mana are words in New Zealand English, borrowed intact from te reo Māori.

According to widely accepted meanings, mana and tapu seem quite distinct concepts, but in fact both relate to the 'power of the gods' (Barlow, 1992) and how this power influences the lives of people, which is why they are bracketed together. This grouping is also a deliberate attempt to disrupt the usual flow of Western-style analyses. Soon after contact the concept of tapu was assimilated to the Christian sense of sacred or holy, and the 'power' aspect of its meaning lost in dominant understandings. Even short and apparently simple definitions such as 'power of the gods' run up against the limits of translation. The English phrase 'power of the gods' has misleading overtones. Not only the concepts themselves, but definitions and explanations must be considered with appreciation of holistic Māori conceptions of reality. The history of academic scholarship on Māori thought and culture clearly demonstrates how often distortions arise, when concepts are separated from each other and from the cosmogenic narratives.

Mauri, hau

Mauri is often translated as 'life principle' in the sense of the Māori belief that all things are living. Mauri is best approximated by the word 'essence' and hau relates to the movement of spiritual energies through associated objects. Mauri in relation to individual people can also be thought of as 'spiritual/psycho-emotional health' that needs to be cared for and can be affected by whatever ails or pleases the person. The concept of mauri is also used in relation to features of the natural environment, such as a river or lake, which are seen as living in Māori conceptual frameworks, since they support life. Māori environmental concerns are therefore often expressed in terms of enhancing or healing the mauri of a particular place.

Hau has been at the centre of an interesting and longstanding debate in anthropology ever since it featured in a seminal book on 'gift theory' by Marcel Mauss (1990). Mauss drew on earlier data in the shape of informant quotes originally collected and published by Elsdon Best (2005) about 'hau ngāherehere' (hau of the forest) and 'hau taonga' (hau of the gift), which Mauss took to mean 'the spirit of the gift' – arguing that in Māori thought, a gift carried some kind of spiritual force wanting to return to its original owner. Mauss went wrong because he was focusing on the gift object itself, but in Māori thought the gift is a symbol of a relationship between people. Giving and receiving of gifts is therefore a metaphor for the spiritual energy of those relationships (Stewart, 2017a).

Utu

Utu is widely understood to mean 'revenge', but this translation is inadequate: it fails to capture the essence of the Māori concept, while reinforcing Eurocentric views of Māori as bloodthirsty savages. Utu is an important Māori philosophical concept that most closely translates as balance, its meaning somewhat like the 'yin-yang' concept of Chinese philosophical traditions.

Whanaungatanga

Whanaungatanga literally means 'kinship' or 'relationship' and defines a person's place within whakapapa, in the social network of whānau, hapū and iwi. The word whanaungatanga is made by adding the suffix 'tanga' (equivalent of -ship) to 'whanaunga' meaning relation, which in turn derives from whānau or family (both nuclear and extended). Whanaungatanga is more generally used meaning 'relationships' as an ethical principle derived from whakapapa, to guide decisions in our interactions with other people in our communities, workplaces and so on. An ethic of whanaungatanga can be extended to guide all human interactions with other denizens of the earth, such as trees, plants and animals (Patterson, 2000). An ontology anchored by whakapapa leads to an ethics of whanaungatanga, operationalised as guidelines of practice in the form of manaakitanga (see next paragraph), and kaitiakitanga (explained above on page 88).

Manaaki, manaakitanga

Manaakitanga is usually translated as hospitality, even as used in the term 'hospitality industry', but this distorts the Indigenous concept to fit within modern economic frameworks of thought and practice. Manaaki combines the two words mana (see above) and aki (exert or encourage), so refers to practices that uphold mana. Adding the suffix 'tanga' switches emphasis from a particular act or situation to the general quality of attention to mana in relationships. The mana of a host group is maintained and enhanced through generosity towards visitors, which is why manaakitanga has come to be equated with hospitality. A more authentic understanding of manaaki as linked to mana, however, extends its application to any and all forms of thinking and action that enhances mana. In this sense, taking responsibility for oneself, acting with integrity, treating others with due respect for their mana and caring for the non-human elements of the environment are all examples of manaakitanga (Patterson, 2000).

Aroha

Aroha is the closest Māori equivalent for 'love', but again, the Indigenous concept does not completely match the English term. Not all of the nuances of love apply to aroha, while aroha has layers of meaning that are conveyed in English by words other than 'love' such as sympathy, compassion, nostalgia, open-mindedness and generosity. The word can be broken into aro + hā: aro is described in the subsection below (see page 95) while hā means the breath, a partial synonym for hau. Aroha literally means to follow the breath, which implies attentive care and empathy for self and other: to follow one's heart; go with the flow. Inherent in the concept of aroha is 'a deep comprehension of another's point of view'; an 'unconditional concern and responsibility for others' (Hoskins, 2012, p. 91). Here aroha calls to a larger concept of love, understood as a boundless sense of responsibility for the Other – whoever it is with whom we interact. Responsibility and responsiveness are linked, both part of a concept of aroha that derives from a Māori worldview. Responsibility to others in relationship sits at the heart of a Māori ethics based on Indigenous concepts of whakapapa, mana and manaaki (Hoskins, 2012). Hoskins reasons that Māori politics based on these traditional concepts is a fundamentally relational politics: one which recognises the risk of relating and relates anyway. Such a relationship is an 'enabling binary' in the sense of being the complete opposite of the binary of terrorism, in which 'neither side can really "see" the other' (Dutta, 2004, p. 434). The concept of aroha, understood as an infinite sense of responsibility for the other with whom we are in relationship, is a flexible and aspirational ethical principle.

Some Māori knowledge terms and concepts

Mātauranga, mōhiotanga

Mātauranga is a verbal noun from mātau, with meanings that include to know, appreciate, apprehend, understand and feel certain of. Mātauranga means both knowledge and understanding; it is also used as the equivalent of education. Salmond (1985) defines mātauranga as 'reliable knowledge' and describes it as very similar to mōhiotanga or 'knowledge acquired by familiarity and the exercise of intelligence' (Salmond, 1985, p. 240). Mōhiotanga is a verbal noun from mōhio, which has a similar range of meanings to mātau, including to know, understand, recognise and deduce, and as an adjective, known or familiar, suspicious, wise or intelligent. These days, mātauranga seems to be used for knowledge in more general senses, possibly related to its adopted meaning of education, while mōhiotanga is more often used in reference to one's personal knowledge, though the two words cannot be clearly distinguished.

Wānanga, kura

Barlow (1991) translates wānanga as 'esoteric learning' in reference to the pre-European whare wānanga, or tribal houses of advanced learning, which were set apart from normal living places. If this meaning is taken to refer to knowledge that is distinct from everyday or practical learning, then wānanga takes on shades of meaning related to philosophy. In modern Māori, the term 'whare wānanga' has been appropriated to mean university. More generally, any extended period of learning can be called a wānanga, such as a live-in held for the purpose of achieving a specific (group) learning goal: a writing retreat, preparing for a performance, or as part of an overall programme such as a tertiary programme. Wānanga is also a verb meaning to think deeply, evaluate or theorise. Though less well-known today, the word kura is listed as similar in meaning to wānanga: the term 'kura huna' means 'knowledge of an especially important nature' and 'whare kura' is a synonym for whare wānanga, one of a series of 'whare' phrases for institutes of higher learning, with others including whare maire and whare takiura. In modern Māori, the word 'kura' translates as 'school' in general, though it is not known if this usage derives from the old meaning of kura for knowledge, or from a transliteration of 'school'.

Tohunga, pūkenga

In classic anthropology the word tohunga has often been translated as sage or priest, while in more recent sources it is taken to mean 'a person who is highly qualified in a specialised field' (Metge, 2015, p. 8). Marsden disputes this interpretation, arguing that since the word tohunga derives from tohu, which means a sign or manifestation, tohunga means 'chosen one' or 'appointed one' (Royal, 2003, p. 14). In this sense, tohunga were representatives and mediators of the gods. Marsden delineates various classes of tohunga, including experts in various fields such as carving or tattooing. In such cases Marsden likens the concept to the Greek idea of the muse, for example, a tohunga tāmoko is 'a person chosen by the gods of tattooing and empowered with mana to suit him for this task' (p. 15). Metge notes that 'tohunga has lingering associations in the popular mind with expertise in occult lore and practice' as grounds for preferring its synonym, pūkenga, which is equated with lecturer, scholar or expert. In the online Māori dictionary, Wakareo, meanings given for both tohunga and pūkenga include 'philosopher'.

Aro/whakaaro, hua/whakahua, mahara/whakamahara

These pairs of words illustrate how the causative prefix 'whaka' works to extend the meanings of stem words. Aro has meanings that include to face, favour or attend to something, desire or inclination, and mind or seat of feelings. From this range of meanings, whakaaro translates as think, thought, plan, intention, consider, opinion and understanding. Today whakaaro is the dominant Māori word used for thinking or thought, but the word 'hua' also includes to think, know or be sure of, among its many meanings, while 'whakahua' means to pronounce, quote or articulate. Mahara is another word that means to think or remember, as well as intestines, and related words maumahara mean memories (mau meaning 'to hold') while whakamahara means to remind or commemorate. Whakamaharatanga and whakamaumaharatanga are dominant Māori words for 'memorial' – showcasing how longer Māori words are made up of several prefixes and suffixes added onto conceptual stem words. Not only the words but the meanings are so co-constructed, in populating the conceptual frameworks of Māori philosophy.

Ako/whakaako, mārama/whakamārama

Ako can mean either teach or learn, and has become widely used in educational discourse, where it has been taken as evidence of democratic Māori ideas about education, in the claim that Māori make no distinction between 'teaching' and 'learning'. I believe this is a mistaken interpretation that has become embedded in national policy: in te reo Māori, the intended meaning, either teach or learn, is made clear by the linguistic context, but such semantic distinctions are obscured in the politicised environment of Māori education. Whakaako means only to teach, which supports this point, since if ako really did mean both teach and learn, then so would whakaako. Mārama has a literal meaning of light and a metaphorical meaning of clear, plain and easy to understand, while whakamārama means to explain.

Ariā, huatau, tautake

These three 'knowledge' words have been adopted in Māori-medium education discussions, though they are not yet standardised and so are not always used consistently. Ariā is the most widely used of this triplet: it has meanings that include idea, concept, theory and hypothesis, though it seems likely these meanings have been extrapolated from its original meaning of resemblance, effect, 'be seen indistinctly' or imaginary presence. Huatau has meanings similar to whakaaro, including thought or to think, idea, opinion or realise, though it also has meanings similar to 'tau' in the sense of comely, suitable, elegant, smooth running and free flowing.

Tautake is listed as meaning either fulcrum or philosophy, which can be understood as literal and metaphorical reference to that which is central or essential in an activity or situation. Tautake combines two words – tau and take – each with many meanings. Tau, in addition to the above meanings, means to settle or come to rest, while 'take' means base or root, reason or cause. One example of the use of 'tautake' in public discourse is a strand of the curriculum for Pūtaiao (Science) in Te Marautanga o Aotearoa (Ministry of Education, 2008), the national statement of curriculum policy for Māori-medium schools, which includes a strand called *Ngā Tautake Pūtaiao me ngā Kōrero-o-Mua*, meaning 'science philosophies and histories'.

Māori philosophy and Western knowledge

The specific knowledge problem inherent in this book is whether it is an *exposition of* Māori philosophy, which therefore works to bring Māori philosophy further into the 'light' of Western knowledge, or, conversely, whether it argues that Māori philosophy cannot be assimilated into Western knowledge. The metaphors we use for knowledge reveal our thinking. To talk about bringing Māori philosophy into the 'light' of Western knowledge is an obvious reference to the European Enlightenment that ushered in the age of science and discovery, which in turn fundamentally shaped the contemporary world. To refer to the 'assimilation' of knowledge is a metaphor from the colonising language of cultural assimilation, which is a dominant though under-theorised theme in the history of post-European Māori experience. While the relatively civilised norms of late British colonialism greatly reduced (compared to other British settler nations such as Australia) the physical violence to which Māori were subjected in the history of the formation of New Zealand, Māori culture and language were fair game for the colonising machine, and were treated to sustained government campaigns of symbolic violence. But to understand Māori today it is important to understand the nuances of variation between the intercultural relationships in the diverse ex-colonies. Right from the start the British colonial intention was never to exterminate Māori, but rather to assimilate Māori, which entailed a philosophical extermination. To write this book is an act of scholarly protest and resistance against the sustained attack posed by colonisation on my *philosophical rights* to think Māori, to think as a Māori and to think with Māori cognitive resources.

The resolution to this conundrum lies in accepting the multiple-faceted nature of the identities all human beings are inherently capable of sustaining. Whatever else may make us different from other people and unique as individuals, we are all descendants of Ranginui and Papatūānuku, all inhabitants of one world, our spaceship planet Earth. It seems reasonable to say all human beings have 'knowledge rights' to all human cognitive resources. In Aotearoa New Zealand we have to overcome the colonising ideologies that have been embedded in the national mind as 'truth-myths' about our national history: no 'full-blood Māori' left alive; Māori conceded the country to Pākehā in the Treaty of Waitangi; Māori are better off for colonisation and so forth. Underneath all of these ideas lies a more fundamental attitude that 'Māori' belong in the past and should cease to exist, the sooner the better. The political motivations and effects of these ideologies results in the need for Māori philosophy as an inherently politically aware tradition and a modification of, rather than a full replacement for, the standard scientific accounts of knowledge. My view of Māori philosophy is as a liminal version of philosophy that inhabits the borders rather than the centre of institutional and academic philosophy: more interested in boundaries between, rather than separatist claims to, intellectual and real territory.

The following chapter presents applications of my version of Māori philosophy in writing about specific topics and events in historical and contemporary Māori education.

Questions for discussion or research

- Discuss the assertion that the Western academic disciplinary structure reflects a Eurocentric worldview. If so, what would be the implications? Can you find examples or evidence to either support or contradict this idea – or both?
- Some Māori knowledge concepts bear some resemblance to certain ideas associated with recent radical movements in Western societies such as New Age, Ecosophy or alternative medicine. Find some examples of such concepts, and discuss why such resemblances might exist. Are such conjunctions likely to be favourably viewed by Māori (or other Indigenous) people? Why, or why not?
- Can you find examples of when Indigenous knowledge could be argued to give a superior account to that of science?

Writing with Māori philosophy

This chapter explores the role of stories and narrative genres in elaborating examples of the clash between Māori and Pākehā cultural worldviews. These examples are like case studies in which Māori philosophy informs the theoretical framework or paradigm underpinning the analysis of specific topics and debates in the history of Māori-Pākehā interactions, especially but not only within education systems.

The first section is an adapted extract from a journal article I co-wrote with Māori colleagues to explore the significance of pōwhiri (formal welcome ceremonies) in academic life in Aotearoa New Zealand (Stewart, Tamatea, & Mika, 2015). These appropriated cultural displays are a fruitful context for exploring the gaps between Māori and Pākehā views on the embedding of 'bicultural' practice within public life. I draw on literary fiction in the form of the classic short story *Parade* by leading Māori author Patricia Grace (1986), and previous literary and social science analyses of this story.

The second section is an adapted extract from a journal article in which I undertake Māori feminist analyses of the censorship of a junior school picture book *Washday at the Pā*, which generated a controversy that has itself become a famous story in national accounts of art, politics and education in Aotearoa New Zealand (Te Papa Tongarewa, 1998).

The third section presents three previously unpublished original short stories, which take further the potential of narratives to tell cultural truths and highlight the incommensurability between Māori and Pākehā worldviews that lies at the heart of any claim for Māori philosophy.

Pōwhiri in education and academia in Aotearoa New Zealand

Through symbolic displays such as pōwhiri (rituals of formal encounter) and tangihanga (funereal rites) Māori people exercise their right to assert cultural difference from the dominant Pākehā or mainstream culture of Aotearoa New Zealand. Clearly, such practices are an extrapolation of Māori traditions and an adaptation to contemporary conditions: by definition, they are hybridized cultural forms (Bhabha, 2009). Guided by the principles of Kaupapa Māori research (Smith, 2003), this analysis draws on Māori philosophy to investigate the increasingly popular practice in the local academy of holding a pōwhiri at the start of an event such as a conference.

In Māori philosophy, stories are useful for their ability to adequately represent Indigenous worldviews (Keown, 2013). According to Thomas King (2003), stories 'are wondrous things. And they are dangerous' (p. 9). The wondrous nature of stories is self-evident, but to call stories 'dangerous' warrants explanation. The 'danger' of stories is their radical teaching power: their ability to disrupt dominant discourses, to capture the nuances of complex educational scenarios. This ability is dangerous because it is critical and creative, transgressing traditional Eurocentric hierarchies of economic and social power.

Māori ambivalence about performing their cultural traditions to serve Pākehā purposes is the topic of a celebrated short story by Māori author Patricia Grace (1986), titled 'Parade'. The central character, Matewai, has gone away to university, but returns to her childhood hometown to take part in her whānau kapa haka during carnival week. There, she is stricken by a new sense of being put on display for the Pākehā audience, suddenly feeling that she and her whānau are like animals in a zoo, clowns in a circus or artefacts in a museum, realisations catalysed by her time spent in the outside world, which has caused her to lose her former innocence and unselfconsciousness (Tawake, 2000). Her elders understand and accept her spiritual malaise, without the need for an explanation. The kuia endorses her new critical vision, saying, 'This is our job, this. To show others who we are'. These simple statements point to the depth of everyday encounters with the incommensurability of the Māori–Pākehā gap, or ethnic binary, which is invoked to greater or lesser degree, each time te reo Māori me ōna tikanga are included in mainstream public institutions and events (Ahmed, 2000).

In Aotearoa New Zealand, it has become almost mandatory to start an education conference with a pōwhiri – a formal welcome conducted along the lines of traditional Māori rituals of encounter. But what does it mean to include Māori traditions and practices in events held in education and other contemporary non-Māori settings in Aotearoa New Zealand, such as conferences, graduations and other formal occasions organised by a school, university or learned society? To begin a conference with a pōwhiri is considered to display respect for Māori culture, and to affirm the place of Māori people in society. Attendees from overseas enjoy the experience of 'authentic' Indigenous culture, and local attendees (non-Māori and Māori alike) have an opportunity to polish and display their own cultural competence. Opening a conference with a pōwhiri is seen as fulfilling contemporary policies of equity and diversity – a process also known as 'tick[ing] the Treaty box' (Mazer & Papesch, 2010, p. 277); therefore the pōwhiri has a value for the organisers and is in this sense a 'good'.

But for Māori involved in such events, the situation is often not so clear-cut. Such occasions often involve what is colloquially known as 'dial-a-kaumātua': a symbolic performance by Māori elders, who typically have little to do with the event or participants, in front of a group of non-Māori who frequently have little or no comprehension of what is being said and done. But what is actually being 'included' by these versions of traditional Māori customs, and whose interests are being served?

Joan Metge (2010) addresses this question in a book section titled 'Pōwhiri, Tikanga and Kaupapa', noting these words, though common in Māori life, 'barely figured in New Zealand English until the 1980s' (p. 75). The 'dramatic quality' of the pōwhiri attracts an audience including the media, with the result that non-Māori have become familiar with the word, but often hold very little understanding of its real meaning. Explaining the traditional form and purpose of the pōwhiri as introductory to the 'hui proper' (p. 77), Metge observes:

> [A]s non-Māori take an increasing interest in Māori culture, the spotlight has been focused on the pōwhiri to such an extent that at times it is detached from the hui context and its preparatory role forgotten. (p. 77)

It has become standard practice for 'organisers of events and conferences to invite the district's tangata whenua to open proceedings with a pōwhiri' including for book festivals, motorsport events and visits by overseas heads of state. But 'the tangata whenua who conduct pōwhiri in such situations usually have no involvement in what follows and leave the scene once the pōwhiri is over' (pp. 77–78): the definition of 'dial-a-pōwhiri'. The 'dial-a-' joke points to the fact that in such cases the pōwhiri has lost its traditional meaning, becoming merely a 'symbolic acknowledgement' (p. 78) of local tangata whenua. This process goes even further in contexts such as education conferences, in which the roles such as tangata whenua become increasingly removed from their traditional Māori meanings.

For Māori staff being expected to organise or lead tikanga Māori (Māori culture) within non-Māori workplaces and other settings is a burdensome extra duty that does not necessarily count in terms of career advancement, so it is important to understand the deeper significance of this work. By including aspects of our culture in the contemporary milieu, we draw attention to the history of oppression of our people, language and culture, and reassert the right of 'Māori' to exist. To begin an event with a Māori greeting, prayer or song reassures Māori participants that Māori language and culture is welcome. To extend the cultural formality of a welcome event by including karanga, wero or haka pōwhiri inevitably heightens the sense of occasion. The reactions of overseas delegates at such events often suggest that, for them, such experiences are 'priceless'. Difficult aspects must be negotiated, however, by those who take responsibility for such occasions. Such practices are widespread in schools as a way to assist Māori students and their whānau (families) feel a sense of belonging, and in addition to provide a valuable learning experience for the larger school community. Māori teachers take responsibility for making it happen. The tertiary sector has also embraced pōwhiri at the start of courses such as initial teacher education degrees, prompted by expectations that tertiary institutions should strive to ameliorate Māori outcomes for student achievement.

My purpose is *not* to 'explain' pōwhiri: plenty of information of that kind is available (see, for example, Battye & Waitai, 2011; Matenga-Kohu & Roberts, 2006; Mikaere, 2013). The point of this analysis is to use Māori philosophy to theorise the material conditions of pōwhiri as part of contemporary working life for Māori and non-Māori professionals and academics in education in Aotearoa New Zealand. Kaupapa Māori theory is used to guide the normalisation of Māori perspectives, words and concepts: methodological decisions that align with the principles of critical Māori bi-literacy (May, 2012) and Kaupapa Māori research methodology (Smith, 2012).

Opinions about contemporary pōwhiri were canvassed for a Māori Television documentary titled 'Pōwhiri – Welcome, or Not?' (Edwards & Ellmers, 2010) from a number of Māori individuals in the public sector, politics and broadcasting, as well as some working in tourism, making money by enacting Māori culture, including pōwhiri, as a marketable commodity, and a unique point of difference. Most Māori who were interviewed mentioned their ambivalence about pōwhiri being held away from marae or Māori settings, in terms of the danger of pōwhiri being trivialised or compromised, with loss of profound concepts and integrity. Māori politician Shane Jones spoke of his disappointment when Micky and Minnie Mouse were 'accorded status as deserving a traditional Māori welcome' – an occasion generating grotesque images of hongi (touching noses) between a Māori warrior in piupiu and the Disney-costumed characters – and recalled an aunt of his complaining that nowadays, pōwhiri are inappropriately held at the proverbial 'drop of a hat'. For Jones, pōwhiri in the state sector are used to affirm the importance of Māori identity and indigeneity. All those who were interviewed for the documentary acknowledged this positive aspect, with lawyer Moana Sinclair remarking, 'It's got to be a good thing.' The former Human Rights Commissioner (2001–2011) Rosslyn Noonan was unambiguous in stating: 'There can't be any state agency in New Zealand where it's inappropriate to have Māori culture and language reflected in what they do and how they operate.' Yet these statements hint at politically innocent or uncritical views that appear to be oblivious to power relations, and at risk of confusing appearance with reality in relation to Māori engagement. These uncritical views increasingly pertain in the tertiary education sector as well, with many Pākehā academics assuming that a pōwhiri makes an event 'more Māori'. But this thought can also be turned upside down: only if Māori were more central in organising an event would a pōwhiri be inevitable, natural and necessary, without the need to import cultural expertise in the form of a 'dial-a-pōwhiri'.

Including pōwhiri in events such as education conferences risks paradox at multiple levels. To Māori participants, these pōwhiri may seem gratuitous and tokenistic, extracted from their natural settings and shorn of cultural meaning. For tourists and newcomers to Māori culture a pōwhiri may seem quaint: a tourist experience that delights, baffles or offends. The expectation that Māori staff will organise pōwhiri at the behest of their Pākehā colleagues serves to highlight the dissonance of being Māori in a non-Māori dominated world. Significantly, this dissonance is visible now, at a point in time when there is a take (Māori word used in wero): a 'thing' that needs to be discussed (Mika, 2015). In the future, holding a pōwhiri may become so much part of routine in educational events that writing about it in this way would no longer be possible.

The disjunctions of including tikanga Māori in educational institutions are central in the work of Wally Penetito, who invokes the term 'a limited version of te ao Māori' in discussing the rationale for institutional marae, in particular those established by universities (Penetito, 2010, pp. 208–9). It is assumed that such marae will help Māori students and staff 'be empowered and experience active agency within the institution in its entirety', but Penetito notes that achievement of this 'lofty goal' has never been proven (p. 209). The same reasoning applies to pōwhiri in academic conferences. Pākehā might assume that starting with a pōwhiri will encourage Māori to attend and participate in the conference, but this is an innocent or politically uncritical assumption that ignores the artificial nature of a 'dial-a-pōwhiri'. Similarly, from this uninformed outsider perspective, the pōwhiri is in danger of being seen as 'more Māori' than the Māori delegate's discussion of ideas relevant to the conference theme.

Simone Drichel uses the story 'Parade' by Patricia Grace to apply work by Jacques Derrida on deconstructive practice to the Māori–Pākehā scenario. Derrida's deconstructive practice operates through the key characteristic of iterability, by which post-colonial identities are able to escape the fixity of stereotype. In order for deconstruction of colonial hierarchies to proceed, Derrida insists it is necessary to engage with the logic of binary oppositions, which 'must begin with an inversion of the hierarchy into which the terms are locked' (Drichel, 2008, p. 594). Referring to the kapa haka performance at the heart of the story, in terms that also apply to education pōwhiri, Drichel observes:

> More notable even than the fact that the otherness of the colonized can be turned into subjectivity by othering the colonizer is the framing of this reversal by a performative act. (p. 598)

In the context of contemporary Aotearoa New Zealand and the Māori experience of assimilation, Drichel offers a warning about the trap of 'neutralization – "We're all New Zealanders"' (p. 595). With this in mind, Drichel argues for the importance of 'a certain emphasis on the otherness of Māori from the dominant (Pākehā) identity, rather than a quick-fix universalism' (p. 595). The education pōwhiri might be a case in point of this 'emphasis on the otherness of Māori' and the performative iterability of hybrid cultural identities.

Contemporary understandings of identity build on fundamental concepts such as these explained by Derrida, which see post-colonialism as an ongoing process of deconstructing the colonising binaries and power hierarchies. This process of deconstruction involves using these ideas to significantly re-read and re-think assumptions and attitudes about social interactions and situations, such as education pōwhiri. Judith Butler's (2010) concept of 'performativity' in identity acknowledges the agentive performative nature of ethnicity. Performativity and the fluidity it offers is also key to Homi Bhabha's (2009) concept of hybridity: less interested in what identity is, and more interested in what identities are for, and what identities can do. These concepts suggest the Māori–Pākehā ethnic binary is best understood as a relationship, rather than a set of categories. Bhabha's term for this positive potential of cultural hybridity is the third space, in which cultural difference is kept in play as a productive tension, and which 'explores the spaces in-between fixed identities through their continuous iterations' (Drichel, 2008, p. 605).

Iterability is central to 'both Judith Butler's performativity and Homi Bhabha's hybridity' (Drichel, 2008, p. 601). Derrida's notion of iterability refers to the plasticity of 'the sign' or symbolic culture, which can be reproduced in ways that are not only recognisable versions of the same, but also infinitely adaptable and new. Informed by this notion of iterability, critical indigeneity recognises the positive potential made available in specific cultural binaries that, crucially, exist within the matrix of time, in a 'complex relationship to temporality' (Drichel, 2008, p. 589). This complex relationship includes multiple temporal dimensions, from the epochal time of sociocultural change, to the biological time of a person's life, to the programme of a single event such as an education conference.

Contemporary Māori identity is (or has potential to be) a critical indigeneity, a radical cultural hybridity, with an aspect of performativity that entails temporality, since agency is located 'in the moment' of the re-enactment of otherness. For this reason, enactment of Māori culture always surfaces the ethical question of acknowledging the Other (the capital 'O' signals the theoretical nature of this entity), hence bringing into view the historically contingent discourses of colonising power (Dutta, 2004, p. 439). The irony of 'organising pōwhiri' being part of someone's job description can hardly be overstated. The nature of education pōwhiri and how they mostly operate reaffirms the assumption that Māori are cultural, traditional and 'outside of time', whereas the participants in the conference 'proper' are intellectual, modern, 'in time' and official. The question that remains is whether some visibility of Māori culture in such events, albeit problematic, is better than none at all.

Temporality entails (among other things) a trajectory into the future, which inserts the possibility for change: it produces the iterative 'ethical moment' of engagement, open to the 'possibility of the unforeseeable' (Drichel, 2008, pp. 608–9). The central role played by temporality in this performative understanding of cultural hybridity invokes the ethics of Levinas, for whom 'time is the ultimate other' (Drichel, 2008, p. 589). This argument serves to clarify and emphasise what is at stake when conference organisers ask their Māori colleagues to organise a pōwhiri.

The above discussions remind us that the need and point of ethnic performativity in the contemporary milieu goes far beyond a checklist or binary question: Is the conference having a pōwhiri, or not? Ethnic identities are as vulnerable as any other form of culture to the dehumanising managerialism of neoliberal reform, with its requirements for paper trails and measurable outputs (Roberts, 2013; Roberts & Peters, 2008). Assessing the ethical quality of what happens in any situation cannot be simply read off the programme (did the conference start with a pōwhiri, or not?). In these rapidly changing times, many Māori involved in education and the public sector share an uncomfortable awareness that the more Māori traditions become 'business-as-usual' for institutions such as universities, the greater the risk to the integrity of Māori culture, as the documentary discussed (Edwards & Ellmers, 2010). The 'otherness' of Māori goes far beyond holding a pōwhiri in a conference programme. A wider view encompasses aspects such as marae within schools, universities and other institutions; the Māori electorates; and the status of te reo Māori as an official national language. The idea of emphasising 'otherness' or Māori difference echoes the Kaupapa Māori use of 'strategic essentialisms', borrowing the words of Gayatri Spivak (cited in Hoskins, 2012, p. 85). So where does this 'strategic otherness' begin and end, and where does it shade into indigeneity, or the right of Māori simply to be Māori?

These open-ended and ineffable questions underpin Te Kawehau Hoskins's argument that Levinasian ethics apply to Māori, since they rest on a relational sense of infinite responsibility to the Other, who 'is unknowable and irreducible to my comprehension and any unity' (Hoskins, 2012, p. 91). This line of thought begs a further difficult question: If the true value of a pōwhiri at the start of an academic conference is to remind the dominant 'business-as-usual' global culture of the existence of the Other, does it matter exactly *what* is said, *who* says it, and all the other detailed questions Māori participants might have about such an occasion?

This reasoning clarifies the distinction between Māori and Pākehā attitudes towards pōwhiri: different motivations, different criteria by which to assess such an event, different responsibilities. It surfaces the detailed content of difference between Pākehā and Māori subjectivities, which could never be erased, other than by supreme force. Under current expectations in tertiary education, non-Māori and Māori education academics alike are caught in a trap in relation to pōwhiri of the 'damned if you do, damned if you don't' variety.

The documentary on pōwhiri concluded that deeper discussions are in order about the role of Māori culture in Aotearoa New Zealand society today (Edwards & Ellmers, 2010). Critical examination of cultural politics in the contemporary milieu is bound to reveal the infinite and paradoxical nature of intercultural relationships (Ahmed, 2000). This quality of 'infinity' ultimately calls to love as a boundless sense of responsibility for the Other – whoever it is with whom we interact. Responsibility to others with whom we are in relationship sits at the heart of a Māori ethics based on traditional concepts of whakapapa, mana and manaaki (Hoskins, 2012). Hoskins argues that Māori politics based on these traditional concepts is a fundamentally relational politics: one which recognises the risk of relating, and relates anyway. Such a relationship can be thought of as an 'enabling binary' and the total opposite of the binary of terrorism, in which 'neither side can really "see" the other' (Dutta, 2004, p. 434).

Can this notion of love as infinity overcome the incommensurability inherent in the Māori–Pākehā ethnic binary? Hoskins (2012) cites Māori scholars and elders including Cleve Barlow, Eddie Durie and Māori Marsden, who reason that inherent in aroha – the nearest though by no means exact Māori equivalent of the word love – is 'a deep comprehension of another's point of view', an 'unconditional concern and responsibility for others' (p. 91). This is why when, as Māori, we organise or take part in Māori culture within non-Māori settings, we must always remember to act with aroha: understanding this work as a gift we offer to ourselves (that is, to other Māori) as well as to non-Māori.

Like ethnicity, aroha and relational ethics, research and writing also involve performative aspects, and interact with many of the ideas discussed above. The temporal aspect of this work has already been noted: there is a point to it now that may not exist in time to come. The inclusion of original narratives and untranslated Māori texts is guided by principles of Kaupapa Māori research. New modes and forms of research hold the possibility of opening up new pathways for critical Māori scholarship to follow further, in future work still to be done. This analysis of pōwhiri challenges the ways institutions frame Māori culture, within programmes and meanings in which Māori are subjugated. It issues a challenge to academics and others to think about the effects of making pōwhiri part of everyday practice in our public institutions, such as schools and universities.

The controversy over *Washday at the Pā*

The *Washday at the Pā* affair is an outstanding example of book censorship in the national history of Aotearoa New Zealand, likened to a 'modern form of book-burning' (Westra, 1964, Publisher's Note, p. 1), which is a phenomenon associated with totalitarianism and not with peaceful democratic nations like Aotearoa New Zealand. The subsequent fame of the author and photographer Ans Westra and the book's dramatic story have meant that this history has stayed alive in national consciousness and has featured in many discussions related to national identity and local art and literature (Ihimaera, 1985; Te Papa Tongarewa, 1998).

Little educational scholarship has been published about *Washday at the Pā* – Roger Openshaw being the most prominent education researcher to write about it (Openshaw, 2001, 2005). Censorship is the dominant theme of published scholarship about the *Washday* controversy, as followed by Openshaw, who takes a social studies perspective to read the decision to withdraw *Washday* from schools as a deplorable example of the government giving in to Māori protest (Openshaw, 2005). But his argument rests on accepting his claim that *Washday* was an accurate portrayal of Māori life, and therefore of value as a school text. This claim rests in turn on the politically suspect assumption that 'Māori life' is a 'natural category' for scientific study, thus bringing in the Kaupapa Māori research argument, as famously espoused by Linda Tuhiwai Smith in her seminal text, *Decolonizing methodologies* (L. T. Smith, 2012)(2012).

Openshaw's argument falls on two points of logic: first, *Washday* was intended as an engaging reader for primary students, not as a sociological text; secondly, the text Westra wrote to accompany her photographs in

Washday can hardly be said to rest on 'accurate' observations of the subjects. In keeping with his argument that the *Washday* controversy showed Māori have 'too much power' Openshaw downplays the importance of the photographs, which he describes as 'profusely illustrat[ing]' (2005, p. 32) the book. But this move further contradicts his argument about scientific or truth value, since by demoting the photographs he implicitly promotes Westra's accompanying storybook text, which is patently inaccurate in terms of how the family would actually have spoken during the time Westra spent with them.

My purpose is to review and comment on previous scholarship about the *Washday* affair, especially the chapter by Barbara Brookes (Brookes, 2000) in her edited collection on the history of (European) houses in Aotearoa New Zealand, and my previous article on *Washday* as an event in the history of Māori education (G. Stewart & Dale, 2016). This research introduces a critical Māori dimension lacking in previous scholarship about *Washday* and draws on the overlap between critical feminism and Kaupapa Māori theory: the territory of Mana Wahine as a theoretical space (Pihama, 2001) in which to understand *Washday at the Pā* as an event about, with and for Māori women.

Mana Wahine means something like the term 'Kaupapa Māori feminism'. The need for Mana Wahine is that even in Kaupapa Māori, Māori women and their views and interests may be sidelined. The principles of Kaupapa Māori research apply equally in Mana Wahine, overlaid with a critical feminist lens. As Naomi Simmonds explains:

> Mana wahine is often understood to be a type of Māori feminism. It extends Kaupapa Māori theory by explicitly exploring the intersection of being Māori and female and all of the diverse and complex things being located in this intersecting space can mean. At its base, mana wahine is about making visible the narratives and experiences, in all of their diversity, of Māori women. (Simmonds, 2011, p. 11)

The decision to withdraw *Washday* from schools was a significant victory for Māori power and Mana Wahine, given that the call for its withdrawal was led by the Māori Womens Welfare League (MWWL).

My interest in adopting Mana Wahine theory here arises from the details of the story itself, about a Māori woman and her children, their encounter with a young Dutch woman with a camera, and the role of the MWWL in having the book withdrawn. This work attends to the importance of the *Washday* history within the larger battle for Māori control over the representation of Māori in the public sphere (McDonald, 2012). The *Washday* debacle was undoubtedly a significant event in this longer-term struggle that impacted in various discursive domains, including educational publishing. This struggle is part of a larger struggle over symbolic power, in which critical Māori scholarship can help shift thinking from Eurocentric towards analyses that take in Māori-centric perspectives. I use Mana Wahine as an Indigenous feminist philosophical methodology to investigate the story of *Washday at the Pā.*

He reo wāhine: Women's voices

In an attempt to bring forward and give life to the voices of women who were involved in the controversy or commented on it, this short section presents quotes and extracts from literature in the form of a conversational script, as if it is the women speaking. This section sets a horizon of discourse based on women's sensibilities about the controversy, in preparation for the Mana Wahine analysis to follow.

Ans Westra: As a teenager I had a stepfather who owned a Leica camera, and he had taken a lot of photographs. That exposed me to photography. We went to see the Family of Man exhibition which made a big impression on me the enjoyment, the variety of people. I also found I had an affinity with photography, I could express more with it than with anything else. And when I came to New Zealand in 1957, I felt I wanted to do a book on the Māori. The books that came out on the Māori were very much aimed at the tourist market very, very formal and posed. So my pictures were more natural ones and stood out that way. I was wanting to observe life as it happened, without interrupting it as much as possible. I had taken some photos of the Māori when I was hitchhiking around I was just trying to see more of the country. Eventually, I thought I would be better off having a car, so I stayed in paid employment until I could afford a car. I wanted to have more freedom. I slept in the car and moved about with it.

I happened to come across this family that looked very picturesque, and I took the photos and took them home, wrote the story and then just presented it [to School Publications] as a total thing. And they didn't change much except they added one photo of the house the family was meant to be moving into, the Māori Affairs house, because they felt that the house that they were living in was sub-standard conditions and it could offend the Māori. Māori were wonderful to photograph because they're just spontaneous and natural, just the most colourful and interesting thing in this country at the time. The booklet was never meant to portray a typical Māori family. It is just the story of a happy family living in the country. It shows the warmth of family relationships (extracts from Art New Zealand, 2016).

Ans Westra (being interviewed in 2011): Even today, as I celebrate 50 years working as a freelance photographer, *Washday at the Pā* remains the highlight of my work. Of course it is my vision of New Zealand that I am putting on film, but it might make people see that certain things are more valuable than they thought they were ... there is great value in the simple way of life with only newspapers on the wall for wallpaper and a scrupulously clean scrubbed kitchen and a lot of *love*. ... I was recording those things as being works of art – the people and the lifestyle. I was over-romanticising it as well, of course. (Westra & Amery, 2011, p. 2 & p. 39, emphasis in original)

Barbara Brookes: In the controversy that erupted over *Washday at the Pā*, Māori women acted both to conserve specific social meanings in the name of tradition and to embrace a modernity enjoyed by white society, while many Pākehā (non-Indigenous) commentators devalued the trappings of modernity and expressed longings for the simplicity of rural life. Pākehā longings were infused with a conception of gender thought to be more 'natural' than those being forged in the towns (Brookes, 2000, p. 242).

The MWWL called on a particular version of Māori identity in order to counter what they saw as a damaging picture of Māori life. Their contested claims may be seen as a political project, staking their right to control their own representation. The League presented a necessarily contradictory position by claiming to be the upholders of both modernity and tradition, thus stressing sameness and uniqueness. The League may well have owed its political clout in the early 1960s to its ability to draw on both worlds, since from its inception it combined traditional Māori protocol with Pākehā bureaucratic forms. These gave Māori women a voice of their own, transcending tribal affiliations, and provided the government with a united body to consult. Māori had a long tradition of seeking such unity, and in the early 1960s the League was the most important embodiment of this history. (Brookes, 2000, pp. 256–7)

Māori women debated a picture of themselves within the League and stimulated discussion in the wider Māori community. Pākehā entered this discussion, bringing the' ir own romantic image and domestic baggage into the debate. Shorn of consumer goods, the heart of the home appeared to lie in a mother's love. Yet just as the Māori increasingly left the countryside for the towns, women were increasingly abandoning the home for the workforce. And the urbanization of Māori ensured that the boundaries of Māori/Pākehā identities could no longer be created by mutual exclusion. (Brookes, 2000, p. 257)

From a letter to the Editor of the *Evening Post*, written by *a Māori mother*: I feel I must write to thank the Minister. … I am a Māori and have four children who have never been near a pā. How can they defend themselves from the humiliation of being teased at school? (Westra, 1964, Publisher's Note, p. 4)

From her letter to the Editor of the *Evening Post*, *Wikitoria Bennett*: As a member of the Māori Women's Welfare League I would like to thank the Minister. … the booklet was not suitable for primary schools. … the Māori school child is immediately placed at a disadvantage with his European schoolfellows and becomes the butt of their derision; he refuses to go to school; and so there's trouble all round. This actually happened, and that is why the League was concerned. (Westra, 1964, Publisher's Note, p. 5)

Jacquie Baxter (Māori poet): Confidence and self-respect are the most treasured possessions to which Māori should hold fast. If you threaten a person's confidence you break his legs. If you threaten his self-respect you batter him about the head. This is a bigger problem than land tenure, living conditions, health or education, and is my answer to the question 'What do you think is the biggest problem faced by the Māori today?' I am often asked for the 'Māori point of view' and my first thought is, 'Why don't you know? Is it because you are so busy stating your own point of view?' The experts wish us well, but sometimes I wonder if they know what it is like to be always on the receiving end. (*Otago Daily Times*, 1964)

Patricia Grace (Māori author): Books are dangerous, and here are four things that make books dangerous to Indigenous readers:

1. They do not reinforce our values, actions, customs, culture and identity.
2. When they tell us only about others they are saying that we do not exist.
3. They may be writing about us but are writing things that are untrue.
4. They are writing about us but saying negative and insensitive things which tell us that we are not good. (Cited in Smith, 2012, p. 35)

A Mana Wahine reading of the Washday controversy

Washday and its history combine to create a story brimming with binaries and paradox, making it a richly educational resource, whose pedagogic potential has been acknowledged but has yet to be fully explored (hence this article, and undoubtedly other work still to come). Three important binaries or hyphens invoked by the *Washday* photographs are: Māori-Pākehā, rural-urban and female-male. Wealth, education and all the power of 'social class' combine to create the sub-text to these divisions between different sections of the population. 'Mrs Wereta' and her children are portrayed living apparently happily on the weaker side of all these power gradients: outside the economy, staying home from school, caught in a time warp, off the grid.

Young, innocent and free of the colonizing baggage internalised by most Kiwis in 1964, Westra saw the sociocultural divide between Māori and Pākehā with sharp clarity. Innocence lent Westra a purity of vision that enabled her to capture romance, even religiosity, 'a spiritual realm of joy and grace' (McDonald, 1988, p. 21) in the photographs she took for *Washday*. Photographing Māori aligned with her existing interests, and their marginalised status perhaps reflected Westra's own sense of being an outsider in her newly adopted country. Referring to Māori as the 'most interesting thing in this country at the time' was a backhanded but pointed insult to Pākehā and Pākehā culture. Westra refers to 'love' in describing the *Washday* family. That she considered it the highlight of her career, despite the distress caused her by the controversy, is testament to the strength of her love for this body of her work.

The educational value of the story of *Washday* lies in its controversial, thought-provoking nature. The powerful nature of the story turns around the recognition of the sense in which Grace argues books are 'dangerous' for Māori and Indigenous readers (see quote in previous section). That many Māori protested against the book, while many Pākehā protested against its destruction, points to the gap between Māori and Pākehā cultural worldviews and cross-cultural understandings. The *Washday* story offers a rich resource for reflecting on national identity in Aotearoa New Zealand: 'an examination of the contours of *Washday* at the Pā is still instructive' (McDonald, 1988, p. 23). Metaphors abound: *Washday* is an 'artistic touchstone', a 'lightning rod for discussion', a 'barometer of cultural outlooks' (Westra & Amery, 2011, p. 2).

But unease and rejection of the controversy – a desire to resolve or 'fix' the dispute between Māori and Pākehā views of *Washday* – is clearly evident in Pākehā commentary. This desire is evident in the two quotes below, taken from notes published in the 1964 Caxton edition of *Washday*, and the 2011 Suite version (suggesting Westra shared these views, or at least approved of their publication):

[T]he Publishers present this Note, and the book itself, in the hope that the controversy and its causes might now be considered more calmly and fruitfully. (Westra, 1964, Publisher's Note, p. 1)

Taika Waititi's *Boy* [is] a movie the Listener recently said spoke 'so truly of our Kiwiness and our certainty that we can now celebrate it'. It would be nice to think we can now say the same of *Washday*. (Westra & Amery, 2011, p. 40)

While these quotes could possibly be read as supporting the assertion that the controversial nature of the *Washday* story is to be valued, this reading seems unlikely, given the tone and context of the full texts from which the two quotes are taken. Furthermore, the second quote is ironic given the criticism of *Boy* by leading Kaupapa Māori and Mana Wahine scholar, Leonie Pihama, who points out how it reproduces all the negative Māori stereotypes of *Once Were Warriors*, albeit with less graphic violence, and situated in a rural coastal setting (Pihama, 2012).

Pākehā inability to understand the Māori objections to *Washday* recalls the argument by Alison Jones, in relation to cross-cultural pedagogy, 'that the valued practices of non-discrimination, freedom, sharing, "knowing each other", can be seen as an embrace of ignorance of difference'; as a 'refus[al of] the possibility of margins to their knowing' (A. Jones, 2001, p. 286, emphases in original). Jones asks, 'Do we [Pākehā] have a cultural incapacity to recognize that we assume we can know (everything)?' (p. 288). Jones's candid excavation of the 'passion for ignorance' (p. 286) that is displayed when Pākehā do not know (understand) Māori, and resist knowing that they do not know, can be compared with Baxter's retort on being asked for the 'Māori point of view': 'Why don't you know?'

The answer to Baxter's wry question about Pākehā ignorance can be found in Brookes's discussion of New Zealand (Pākehā) identity, using the terms devised by Lawrence Jones (1989) in his synopsis of the history of New Zealand literature and identity: starting with the Pastoral Dream, building on its foundations a welfare state version of the Just City, later converted into the Affluent Suburb.

Māori disrupted this Dream, were excluded from the Just City, and denied entry to the Affluent Suburb. Pākehā identities were dependent upon this exclusion. (Brookes, 2000, p. 244)

If Pākehā identity depends on excluding Māori, it is unsurprising that Pākehā do not know in detail how Māori view the world. Pākehā ignorance of Māori thinking is also in keeping with the sociological rule that, in any society, members of powerful groups have the privilege of remaining ignorant (if they so choose) about disempowered groups, while the powerless have every reason to study the powerful (Graeber, 2012). Contemporary calls for more truthful versions of the national history of Aotearoa New Zealand to be taught in schools, and for national commemoration of the nineteenth-century Land Wars (Smallman, 2016) continue this contestation over national identity, which changes terms over the years, as questions of Māori difference shift increasingly towards more symbolic realms, such as books and imagery.

I consider Brookes' chapter (2000) a more feminist reading, more critical than either of the accounts included with the second and third *Washday* revisions, or those of Openshaw (2001, 2005). To a greater extent than Openshaw, Brookes acknowledges the significance of the work MWWL were doing in the 1960s to help Māori women and children, and the way *Washday* unwittingly undermined this work. Brookes insightfully notes how MWWL played both cultural cards, and the role of 'gender' in the affection for *Washday* expressed by many non-Māori commentators. Brookes explores gender issues in the nostalgic comments on familial happiness that many saw in *Washday*: 'the photographs almost conveyed the appetising smell of Mrs Wereta's home-made bread' (Brookes, 2000, p. 255).

But towards the end of her chapter, Brookes seems to go off track, saying:

> The picture of Māori life that appeared in *Washday at the Pā* differed little than earlier school journals. But, by the 1960s, the equation of domestic modernity with social worth was such that the League could

only be outraged at a depiction of Māori as pre-modern. (Brookes, 2000, p. 255)

The first sentence seems at odds with the stress on Westra's photographs of Māori as being unlike the usual imagery of the times. Certainly the images in *Washday* are very different from those in the classic school journal, *Life in the Pā* (Chapman-Taylor, 1948), which was reprinted more than once and still common in classrooms in the 1960s. The problem with the second sentence is that the *Washday* depiction of Māori life is *not* pre-modern: it is an outdated, impoverished form of the modern. 'Pre-modern' aptly describes the depiction of Māori life in *Life in the Pā*.

Brookes reasons that MWWL's victory over *Washday* was an indication of their strength as a political lobby group and their effectiveness as an emerging new form of Māori leadership. She stresses the significance of the united, pan-tribal nature of MWWL, and their ability to draw on both cultures to their own advantage. The problem with Brookes's argument, however, although more sympathetic towards the MWWL, and more honest about the sexism that drove much support for *Washday*, is that at base it differs little from that of Openshaw: it seems stuck in lack of comprehension of the Māori view. Brookes ends on an ambivalent note, with a quote from the Listener about two peoples building a nation 'moving forward, but not quite sure where [they were] going' (Brookes, 2000, p. 257).

Mana Wahine does not see the MWWL's victory as resulting from their 'power' in the sense of 'political clout' (Brookes, 2000, p. 257), a concept carrying a shadow image of the Minister of Education 'bowing to the demands of a small pressure group' (Westra, 1964, Publisher's Note, p. 7) to avoid further trouble. If this is the general understanding, if the views in Openshaw (2005) and Brookes (2000) are representative (and it seems they are) then of course, there is every need to object. Who wants to live in a country where 'trouble-making' gets results? The minister for his part seemed unable to articulate a satisfactory explanation for his decision: his statement that 'in matters like this *we* must respect the feelings of *other people*' is telling because of how it displays the 'them and us' thinking so endemic, albeit repressed (i.e. a 'passion for ignorance'), in Pākehā views of their own social conditions (Westra, 1964, Publisher's Note, p. 4, emphases added).

Rather, a Mana Wahine view understands the protest put to the minister by the MWWL in terms of their mana. The women of MWWL experienced or shared the misery these photographs caused for Māori children and their mothers. As a matter of mana, on behalf of all Māori women and children, it was only right and appropriate for them to demand its withdrawal, however unfortunate the waste of resources, and irrespective of its merits. Not to do so would have been remiss, in mana terms. Some of its images were clearly inappropriate for a classroom book. It was simply wrong for such images to be unleashed in classrooms by School Publications acting on behalf of the minister, government and public purse. The right advice was not used during its production. In modern parlance, *Washday* was unfit for purpose. Of course, the mana of the women of MWWL was enhanced following their success. But their actions in the first place were required by their Mana Wahine, which is innate: to take seriously their role as representatives and advocates of Māori families demanded no less.

Mana Wahine is a Māori form of theory (like Kaupapa Māori) that draws on Indigenous Māori culture and practices. Kaupapa Māori has succeeded in part through the use of 'strategic essentialism' which involves 'the simplification of group identity to achieve certain political and social goals' (Hoskins, 2012, p. 85). Likewise, Mana Wahine capitalises on a form of strategic essentialism employed in research, since Mana Wahine does not exist in isolation but is always entangled with mana tane, as well as with all the other forms of mana (Robin, 1991). Mana Wahine is therefore a complex shifting space of intersectionality, in which to engage Māori women as active agents. Mana Wahine is an intervention that enables the story of Washday to be told from a 'wahine-centric' point of view: a term used to draw attention to the nuances of similarity and difference between this and a Māori-centric perspective.

This analysis centres on the views of Māori women and the needs of Māori children, as part of the intended primary school readership of *Washday*. A Mana Wahine reading would surely disagree with the following opinion in the Caxton edition:

> There were, we were told, some actual instances of teasing. Whether they justified the League's request, the Minister's action, and all the consequences, can hardly be determined now. (Westra, 1964, Publisher's Note, p. 8)

This view is ethically unsound since it places the value of a book above the interests of children and their right not to be harmed by the state, which includes its structures such as schooling and schoolbooks.

> Traditionally we have talked about photographs freezing moments in time. In *Washday* they are trapped like an insect in resin. Resin that has the power of a prism: as soon as one view has been shone through *Washday*, a multitude of others have splintered off, presenting a spectrum of perspectives. (Westra & Amery, 2011, p. 2)

Not only the photographs, but the people in the photographs, and the story of the book, are 'trapped like an insect in resin' – like an exhibit in the museum of Māori education history: a valuable, a taonga for us to examine, study and learn from. This section has shone a wahine-centric view through *Washday* to enable a Kaupapa Māori feminist re-reading that solves the puzzle of the controversy. In mana terms, the wāhine (women) of MWWL had no option but to demand the withdrawal of *Washday*. It was a harsh lesson for state publishing, and an unfortunate waste of public resources. But responsibility for that wastefulness must be sheeted home to School Publications, not wrong-headedly attributed to MWWL or Westra, as in the dominant explanations. To research an historical event in education such as the *Washday* controversy can itself be seen as a form of devotion, enacted in the time, effort and careful thought by which such research proceeds. This research stakes a claim for Mana Wahine on the spectrum of perspectives about the controversy: adding to the conversation, rich and surely still unfinished, sparked by this national treasure, the taonga that is *Washday at the Pā*.

Telling truth and stories

This section consists of three original stories that attempt to confront the reader with the kinds of conundrums, paradoxes and juxtapositions that underpin contemporary Māori experience. The stories are based on 'honest reporting' of actual experiences, both my own and those of others as told to or reconstructed by me. In each story the focus is on a clash between Indigenous and Western worldviews, and how that clash is played out by ordinary citizens in everyday situations, in one of the most liberal, peaceful contemporary nation-states. In writing these stories I am inspired by the famous Māori authors of my generation, such as Patricia Grace (referred to in the previous section) whose oeuvre epitomises the use of the short story form as a vehicle for critical Māori social commentary. Below are background notes to introduce each of the three stories that follow.

Come and get it!

At only 200 words this story is a mere snippet, no bigger than the baby fish that was its catalyst. Yet in its brevity it is complete – story told, point taken, lunch over. In simple terms such as 'cuzzie', 'the old house', 'Tangaroa', it paints a thumbnail sketch of Māori life and thought that recognises yet stands apart from dominant national norms. It gestures to the depths of intercultural incommensurability between Māori and Pākehā in such banal details as the legal sizes of fish to eat for lunch.

Get a real job

This second brief vignette is a story I was told by my friend Tahau Mahanga, also known as Colin Henry. He is an example of a tradition among Māori families of giving children both a 'real' or Māori name, and a 'school' or English name: a literal 'naming' of the Māori experience of living in two worlds. This story gently probes the hegemony in which previous generations of Māori people accepted their role of providing the manual labour necessary to build the primary industries of farming and forestry upon which the profitability of the modern economy depends. The profits reaped from this land were founded upon its cheap acquisition by confiscation from its original owners, whose descendants later laboured for the new owners, until mechanization made them redundant. This story is about changing personal-social norms between generations, within the larger changes wrought by macro-economic forces on people's lives.

The way of the red mist

This is a more extended attempt to harness the power of stories and genres for Indigenous social commentary. I wrote this story in two parts of contrasting styles to represent two cultural perspectives, Pākehā and Māori, on one event, which is known in national history as 'the haka party incident' (Wikipedia, 2018). Part one is in a reasonably formal style, slightly tongue-in-cheek (such as use of the outdated hybrid plural form 'Māoris'), presenting a version of the 'casual racism' that underpins standard Kiwi culture. In deliberate juxtaposition of styles, Part two is written 'as if' narrated by its protagonist, Mangu, and aims to capture his straightforward Māori way of telling a story.

The events in this story made repeated appearances in my own life, first as a fourteen-year-old schoolgirl in Auckland in the 1970s. I recall my fright when a motorcycle with a scantily dressed male rider suddenly roared up the path behind me, seeming to chase me as I walked my usual lunchtime circuit of the school grounds. Five years later in 1979, I was in the second year of my science degree at university when the 'haka party' incident at the centre of this story took place. I heard about it after it happened, and the following day attended the student meeting in the quad. Only then did I start to understand the motorcycle incident from my school days. Several years after that I was working in a science job in Auckland when I travelled north to attend a family hui mate (funeral). There I met Mangu as my sister's friend from the Waitangi protest movement – a striking individual. I found it hard to judge if he was young or old – he looked both at the same time. A few years later again, by then aged twenty-seven, and having left Auckland and my job and headed north to reconnect with 'my Māori side' I met him again, and this time we eventually became permanently entangled through our son Nuku (named by my father after his father).

Come and get it!

'Come and get it!'

As I slid into my seat and looked at my lunch, my heart gave a small lurch at the sight of the delicate little fried fish, not quite overlapping the sides of my plate from tip to tail. It was a mini version of the snapper I mostly see displayed on ice at the market. I was sure it was a very illegal catch.

'Where did these come from? They're way under.'

'Cuzzie dropped them off – he had a good night out on the river last night, down below the old house – he gave everyone three or four. This is my favourite way to eat snapper – the sweetest.'

'I feel complicit ... guess I won't let it spoil my lunch though ... would be a bigger crime to waste it now.'

'Pāpa used to say the old Māori custom is to eat the little ones, but leave the big breeding fish alone – they are the ones that produce the future generations. When the time is right to eat these panfries, they come up the river in droves – one pass and the net is full. So enjoy – and feel good about working with Tangaroa, even if the Pākehā calls it a crime.'

Get a real job

I began earning money at the age of eleven when my mates and I packed the hall at Tokoroa Intermediate in 1962 for lunchtime concerts, charging threepence a head. After moving to Australia in the seventies, the band played with overseas artists on tour The Commodores, Tina Turner, Dionne Warwick, Osibisa, and with our mates, Dalvanius and the Fascinations.

Mum and I stayed close, no matter how many years I stayed away, but she never ever thought of my music as real work. For her and those older generations of humble Māori people, a job meant forty hours a week, trading your days and muscle power for a weekly pay packet. She never stopped nagging me to give up the band and 'get a real job'. The paper-pulp industries of the central North Island were built on her kind of thinking.

The band got a chance to tour America on the Chitlin' Circuit, but the wives and kids vetoed that move, a wasted chance that ended up affecting the way I saw my life. Later, after my marriage was over, I had some fun years on the cruise ships, playing three hours a night, and eating and drinking for next to nothing the rest of the time.

Mum moved back to Whangarei about 1990, renting a Catholic flat up Tiki Hill. By then the primary industries were becoming mechanized, and jobs were scarce. Once-bustling towns like Tokoroa were now full of boarded-up shops and unkempt streets.

On my visits back between cruises I would stay with Mum, and the Whangarei Hotel publican would get me to play lunchtimes, a guitar party-style solo act. In those years Mum talked a lot about the financial misfortunes suffered by various members of the wider whānau. More and more cousins were languishing on the dole, even skilled tradesmen with families to support. I said I'd never expected the Tokoroa jobs to last forever, and she looked at me with a slightly shocked expression, as if she had never imagined there would be no more 'real jobs' for our people.

One day I had to interrupt her latest tale of family woe to go and get ready to play.

'Who's got a real job now, eh Mum?'

The way of the red mist

Part one

Central Auckland, late summer 1979. In the lower levels of a high-rise building on Symonds St, about fifty young men who are studying engineering are in a classroom, but there are no lectures on today. It is Capping Week, and they are preparing for an activity that is a tradition in their school, which, as they are often reminded, is part of the leading educational institution in the country, one of the world's top-100 universities.

The young men (there are no female engineering students) are almost all Pākehā, and most of them come from family homes in the wealthy eastern suburbs of this, the largest city in the country. Their fathers are also engineers, or doctors, dentists, lawyers or architects, and most of them have devoted stay-at-home mothers. Having achieved highly at their prestigious schools to earn their place on the engineering degree programme, they know they are on the path to becoming highly paid professionals, future national leaders and citizens of influence in this lovely little land of opportunity.

It is the end of the decade of flower power: of Woodstock, LSD and protest against the Vietnam War by a generation who have grown up in the good years of economic boom times and liberal social conditions that followed the recovery after the Second World War. The Western world has seen the horrors of genocide on a previously unimaginable scale, born of a belief in white racial superiority. Those awful memories have slowly faded as a new sense of fairness and respect for human rights have grown up in their place. In this new age of sensitivity and tolerance for different cultures and peoples, New Zealand has gained a strong reputation for 'the best race relations in the world'. This simply reinforced the already widespread belief among Pākehā that everything was fine here, and nothing needed to change.

Certainly, these young men see no reason why their annual Capping tradition should not happen. They are taking off their shirts, and donning rough costumes made from strips of paper and plastic hanging from a string waistband. They are decorating their torsos, limbs and faces with felt pen and shoe polish designs. They are showing each other how they will contort their faces, practising postures involving torso-slapping and stamping, imitating dimly remembered illustrations in schoolbooks.

All these young men know that in the past year, since the last Capping, a couple of Māori students approached the Engineering School wanting to discuss their annual stunt, saying it was inappropriate and disrespectful to their cultural traditions. Perhaps as a university, they argued, we should be setting an example to the rest of society. The university had a responsibility to change its policies, so that not only white young men from wealthy homes and the top Auckland schools were able to become students in its programmes. They believed stunts like the engineers' haka party were out of date in these enlightened times. It was very difficult to get anyone to meet with them, and of course, nobody they did speak with took their views at all seriously.

The students and lecturers alike think that if Māoris want to go to university they have to prove they are up to it. If they are intelligent enough, there's nothing stopping them except their own tendency to be lazy and waste time instead of working. For the vanishingly small number of Māoris (or, more accurately, so they believe, half-castes who take after their non-Māori side) who did make it to university, well, they needed to be able to handle the way things worked in the real world, so what were they complaining about, anyway? There was nothing illegal about dressing up and running around yelling and pretending to be Māori warriors, was there? Talking about it among themselves, they have convinced each other that Māoris should feel flattered the School of Engineering chooses to include their culture in its traditions.

Part two

When I was born at Kaitaia Hospital my mother gave me a flash-sounding name made from the names of the doctors and nurses who helped her to deliver me. A few days later my uncle took one look at me and said, 'Mangumangu taipō' which means 'black goblin'. My name has been Mangu ever since. My life has been hard: you can see that just by looking at me. I never got to go to school much because my parents made us work on the gardens a lot of the time, and we stayed at the marae whenever there was a hui. My father had been to the Second World War where there was something called 'mustard gas' that was said to be the reason so many of his generation died in their fifties, lungs had it. He died when I was ten and Mum died when I was twelve. I was pretty much on my own after that. Call it the university of hard knocks.

When I came back from Australia, I spent a few years travelling around with the kaumātua of our area, as they went from hui to hui at marae all around Te Taitokerau and occasionally further afield, but especially those of Muriwhenua which the Pākehā call 'the Far North'. It was a kind of apprenticeship in te reo me ngā tikanga.

I may not have much education, but I know my whakapapa, and there are no Pākehā in it. This is no big deal to a Māori, but apparently huge for tauiwi, and it has put me in the spotlight a bit. Don Brash had his biggest political moment with his first Orewa speech in 2004, saying that since there are no more full Māori alive there is no longer any reason for Māori seats or policies. The next day the *New Zealand Herald* newspaper sent their reporters in search of a full-blood Māori, and I was the first one they found I was in Auckland at the time, when I got the phone call.

You remember at my sixtieth birthday at the marae in 2009 the whānau also commemorated thirty years since the engineers' haka party? That was a long time before you were even a twinkle in your mother's eye, my boy, so I'll give you a quick rundown on what happened that day.

Your aunty and uncle were at varsity back then; they had made it somehow from their school where they grew up on the poor side of town. They were among the younger members of Ngā Tamatoa, a Waitangi protest group, which is where we saw each other in those days I was working at the freezing works and they were doing BAs. At one of our meetings they told the group about this thing called the 'engineers' haka party', which was a Capping stunt that was a tradition for some of the students at the university. Apparently at Capping time the students got away with stupid shit. These idiots pretended to be 'Māori warriors' as they went on a massive pub crawl around central Auckland.

Over the next few meetings of Ngā Tamatoa your aunty kept updating us on their efforts to discuss putting an end to this racist crap. Finally, in about March the next year, she told us they had been given permission to speak directly to the students themselves and ask them not to go ahead. She asked if anyone could go and support them, so I did, and some of the others. We met up at the pub that used to be on the corner and walked down the street to the place. Your aunty was in charge as usual and briefed us as we went. I remember she looked directly at me as she reminded us there was to be no physical intimidation; we were there to talk, to reason, to make them understand how the political landscape had changed.

Maybe I hadn't listened properly – I thought we were there to talk to them about not going ahead. As we walked into the building I was up the front with your uncle and aunty. We walked down the steps and suddenly in front of me was a big room full of wankers in plastic piupiu, smeared with black vivid. The red mist came down and I charged, smashing the first one I got to. All hell broke loose.

Of course, your uncles all jumped on me and got me pinned down before I could hit more than a few of them. Got me out of there pretty damn quick, and nobody afterwards ever owned up as to who I was. Anyway, the rest is history, and so is the engineers' haka party. I guess you could call it an example of their saying, 'actions speak louder than words'.

Questions for discussion or research

- Research the use of narrative genres (short stories, poems, etc.) in philosophical scholarship.
- Use creative writing to make a scholarly response to a research topic of personal significance.

Making philosophy Māori

This book raises a challenge to Eurocentric scholarship, which is by definition knowledge supported by unsound philosophical commitments. Because of these unsound philosophical supports for the current dominant Eurocentric culture in Aotearoa New Zealand, an indigenous challenge must include engagement at the philosophical level. This is my rationale for writing about Māori philosophy, to advance this challenge from the vantage point of being a 'wild' (or possibly a 'native') philosopher. To put an identity lens such as 'Māori' across a knowledge term such as 'philosophy' (or science, research or education) is to raise the question of difference at a fundamental level and thereby challenge the universalism on which the global (white) academy stands. Through central concepts and worked examples this book is intended to be a kind of textbook about Māori ways of thinking, complete with sufficient personal stories and contextual information to convey the sense of a located, embodied, indigenous thinker-author.

Te kōhatu o te wānanga – philosophy's stone

While I was working on this book I would regularly get up at 'ungodly' hours to write. As an academic I find the quiet darkness of the night supports my creative writing practice and helps my thought processes settle and deepen. The Māori phrase 'te kōhatu o te wānanga' (literally, the stone of the wānanga) came to me during those times of writing the chapters. Reading and thinking about how stones were used in the traditional tribal wānanga houses of learning: the youngster being trained for future duties within the clan related to maintenance of the oral knowledge base; sitting in the dark with a stone in the mouth, listening to the recitations of the elders and tōhunga. The nature of a stone: its symbolic relationship to the planet, the biosphere, the local environment. The stone is a holographic fragment of Papatūānuku; its essence is in contrast with water, air and fire, the other major elements of the non-living world. I thought about the pet pigeons I kept as a child, who swallowed stones to digest their food. The cultural significance of a stone: much has been made of the 'three baskets of knowledge' of Māori traditions, to such an extent that the role of stones in relation to knowledge has been relatively overlooked, just as Māori knowledge has itself been overlooked in the university curriculum: hiding in plain sight, in the liminal space of the intercultural hyphen between languages and cultural worlds. The image of 'te kōhatu o te wānanga' came to symbolise my work of writing this book, as a material artefact and a set of ideas, a small intellectual offering that seeks to contribute to the larger project of Māori decolonisation.

Nō reira kua mutu aku kōrero i konei
Koia tēnei taku kōhatu o te wānanga
He kongakonga o Papatūānuku
Tīhei mauriora
Ka huri[1]

Notes

Chapter 5

1 In the 1950s my mother and Māori Marsden knew one another and had many friends in common from Auckland University social circles. Today his children and grandchildren are part of my personal and family networks.

2 In contrast with 'hau' for wind, or moving air, also related to moving spiritual energies, which like air are omnipresent, but usually go unnoticed.

Chapter 7

1 I have finished what I wanted to say/this book is my philosophy's stone/a crumb of Papatūānuku/greetings to all/the end.

Glossary

Aotearoa	a Māori name for New Zealand
aroha	nearest equivalent to love
atua	deities
haka	war dance
hapū	kin group
hinengaro	modern word for mind
hui	gathering
i	(a participle or connecting word in Māori syntax)
iwi	people, kin group
kaitiakitanga	guardianship, Māori ethics of environmentalism
karakia	incantations, prayer
karanga	call
kaumātua	male elder, elderly
kaupapa	cause, philosophy
kete	flax basket
ki	(a participle or connecting word in Māori syntax)
Kiwi	modern nickname for New Zealander
kōhanga	nest
kōhatu	stone
kōmako	songbird,
kōrero	talk
koru	spiral
kura	school
mana	prestige
Māori	indigenous people of Aotearoa New Zealand
marae	Māori centre of community
mataora	living face
mate	death, illness, problem
mauri	vital essence, object imbued with spiritual power
me	and
ngā	the (plural)
pā	Māori village, defensible encampment
Pākehā	white New Zealander

Papatūānuku	earth mother deity
piupiu	flax skirt
pūtea	funds
Ranginui	sky father deity
reo	language, voice
rua	two
Rūaumoko	deity of earthquakes and volcanoes
tahi	one
takarangi	double spiral motif in carving
tāmoko	tattoo
Tāne	ancestor deity
Tangaroa	deity of the seas
tangata whenua	traditional owners
tapu	sacred
tauiwi	immigrant
tautake	philosophy
Tāwhaki	ancestor deity
te	the (singular)
tikanga	customs, ethics
tinana	body
tohunga	tribal expert
toru	three
utu	balance
wairua	spiritual or non-physical part of a human being
waka	canoe, mode of transport
wānanga	place of learning, live-in, study period
whakaaro	thought
whakapapa	genealogy
whānau	family
whanaungatanga	kin relationships
whare	house, building

Study guide material

Chapter 1: Finding Māori philosophy

Teaching notes

This chapter is the logical place to start teaching this book, and is itself a kind of 'study guide' since it defines the book's key concepts and themes; locates Māori philosophy in relation to the World Philosophies series; introduces the author; and explains the approach taken to writing the book, including the role of the Māori language.

The topic of Māori Philosophy lends itself to the following forms of assessment:

- research assignments – using one of the questions below, or variations thereof;
- annotated bibliography – a useful step towards mastering critical literature reviews;
- classroom debates – with a moot devised perhaps from one of the binaries associated with the topic;
- poster or infographic assignment – for a more creative approach.

Questions for discussion or research

- Investigate the uses of 'global' and 'world' as adjectives or modifiers in various contexts. Do your results support the argument in this chapter that 'global' is associated with capitalist power while 'world' is more fitting for indigenous or folk values?
- Discuss the assertion that European colonisation of indigenous peoples, including Māori, has involved philosophical subjugation, in addition to the more obvious physical aspects of colonising oppression. How does this idea link to that of 'epistemic violence'?

- Consider the premise that any attempt to describe a non-Western philosophy such as Māori philosophy will run up against logical conflicts.

Suggestions for further reading

Jackson, M. (1992). The Treaty and the word: the colonization of Māori philosophy. In G. Oddie & R. Perrett (Eds.), *Justice, ethics and New Zealand society* (pp. 1–10). Oxford, UK: Oxford University Press.

Jackson's chapter is a catalyst and inspiration for the project of writing this book. It is one of the few pre-existing sources that specifically address the topic of Māori philosophy and thus it makes a worthy candidate for extension reading.

Webster, S. (1998). *Patrons of Maori culture: Power, theory and ideology in the Maori renaissance.* Dunedin: University of Otago Press.

Webster is an American by birth who migrated to New Zealand and worked in the anthropology department of the University of Auckland, during which time he wrote about the Māori Renaissance from an outsider's point of view. He was one of the participants in a debate sparked by the publication of the article by Alan Hanson discussed in Chapter 3.

Chapter 2: Theoretical concepts for researching Māori philosophy

Teaching notes

This chapter provides succinct explanations of the key concepts used in the following chapters. It need not be read in sequence in order to understand the rest of the book, but this chapter serves as a convenient reference guide that may be particularly useful for the student reader, and which can be referred to as needed in teaching or studying Māori or indigenous philosophies.

Questions for discussion or research

• What is 'scientism' and what are its various forms? Discuss possible examples of how scientism operates in society and in academia.

• Does science as a knowledge system contain inbuilt paradoxes and limitations? How does the concept of 'scientism' relate to this question?

• Discuss and define the links between the concepts of world view, relativism, incommensurability, and differend.

• Are the above four separate concepts, or is it more accurate to think of them as different levels or versions of the same concept?

Suggestions for further reading

Kearney, M. (1984). *World view*. Novato, CA: Chandler & Sharp Publishers, Inc.

This book-length work focuses on the concept of worldview (which since its publication has become accepted as a single word) and usefully narrates its history, giving an account of the debates from whence it emerged, and why, and its current range of applications.

Herrnstein Smith, B. (2005). *Scandalous knowledge: science, truth and the human*. Edinburgh: Edinburgh University Press Ltd.

This book contains a readable and balanced overview of the longstanding and intransigent knowledge debates between universalism and relativism. In particular, this book explains how a position of weak relativism is not only useful but inevitable for the contemporary twenty-first-century student of human cultures and knowledges, without which the very concept of World Philosophies makes no sense.

Hoyningen-Huene, P., & Sankey, H. (Eds.). (2001). *Incommensurability and related matters.* Dordrecht & Boston & London: Kluwer Academic Publishers.

The contributors to this edited collection vary in their acceptance or otherwise of relativist ideas, and as a whole the book offers a good representation of the universalism–relativism debate. The first chapter by Richard Boyd, titled *Reference, (in)commensurability and meanings: Some (perhaps) unanticipated complexities* (pp. 1–63) offers a nuanced account of why positions of weak relativism make more sense and are more politically acceptable than the still-dominant position in philosophy of opposition on principle to anything other than universalism, despite its inevitable collapse into Eurocentrism.

Chapter 3: Still being Māori

Teaching notes

This chapter begins to articulate key Māori philosophical ideas by exploring Māori thinking about the concept of 'the self' as encapsulated in the cosmogenic narratives and other traditional oral texts. The discussions in this chapter draw on a combination of sources, including published literature, examples found within the Māori language itself, and personal anecdotes and responses, and seek to highlight differences found between the indigenous Māori ideas and those of contemporary globalised Western culture.

Since indigenous identities are place based and localised, to talk about Māori ideas of the self requires movement beyond the level of 'Māori', which is a post-colonial umbrella ethnicity, towards the specificity of the 'iwi' or 'kinship grouping' – this phrase being a more accurate gloss than the apparently pejorative term 'tribe' that was favoured by colonial anthropology. This example shows how undertaking an exploration of indigenous philosophies requires constant vigilance for colonising attitudes built into the very terms of the debate.

Questions for discussion or research

*   Discuss the difficulty of labelling any aspect of indigenous knowledge or experience as 'pure' or 'authentic' in the contemporary milieu, and how this conundrum can be navigated in studying World Philosophies.

*   Indigenous peoples in modern Western societies, such as Māori people in New Zealand, suffer from being both romanticised and vilified in public discourse such as the media. Find and discuss some examples of both these opposing attitudes towards Māori and/or other indigenous groups.

Suggestions for further reading

Rangihau, J. (1992). Being Māori. In M. King (Ed.), *Te ao hurihuri* (pp. 183–90). Auckland: Reed.

This short section by Tūhoe elder John Rangihau is drawn on in this chapter, and makes good further reading on the topic of Māori ideas of the self, along with the rest of the edited collection in which it appears. This classic collection was considered groundbreaking at the time of its original publication in 1975 because although the editor Michael King was a Pākehā historian, all the chapters were written by leading Māori tribal elders and thinkers, including Timoti Karetu, Robert Mahuta, Māori Marsden, Ngoi Pewhairangi and Ranginui Walker.

The references in this book are mainly from recognised academic research literature, but beyond this there is an enormous number and range of books about all aspects of Māori people and culture, written for the general reader. The four titles listed below are recent examples of accessible overview treatments, two by Pākehā authors (James Belich and Don Stafford) and two by Māori authors (Buddy Mikaere and

Pāora Walker). Other authors of readable and well-researched books on Māori topics include Joan Metge, Anne Salmond and Malcolm Mulholland, among many others.

Belich, J. (2007). *Making peoples: a history of the New Zealanders: from Polynesian settlement to the end of the nineteenth century.* Auckland, New Zealand: Penguin.

Mikaere, B. (2013). *Māori in Aotearoa New Zealand: understanding the culture, protocols, and customs.* Auckland, New Zealand: New Holland.

Stafford, D. (2008). *Introducing Māori culture.* Auckland, New Zealand: Reed.

Walker, P. (2007). *Māori: a visitor's guide.* Auckland, New Zealand: Reed.

Chapter 4: Te ao Māori – the Māori world

Teaching notes

This chapter turns to the world as it continues to elaborate and explore the pervasive binaries that characterise Māori experience and thought, both in indigenous traditions and under the contemporary conditions of post-colonialism. In social science, binaries have often come to be regarded as intrinsically bad or wrong, but this chapter argues for the difference between binaries that are reified, which often lead to erroneous conclusions, and those that are natural or inevitable, which are basic cognitive resources in learning and thinking about the world and the place of humans within it. Study of this chapter would therefore be complemented by examining philosophical treatments of binaries more generally.

This chapter includes a brief synopsis of the beginning of the traditional Māori cosmogenic narratives, but more detailed published versions of these stories, usually referred to as 'Māori myths and legends', are widely available (an online collection funded by the New

Zealand government is at www.digitalnz.org – search for 'Māori myths and legends' on the homepage). These narratives are central in building up an account of the Māori world, and the difference between this and Māori experience of the contemporary milieu. As with all the material in this book, useful comparisons can be made with other social contexts, but caution in such comparisons is warranted. It is important to recognise that each society has its own history of relationships between indigenous and settler peoples, and invalid assumptions are best avoided. It is particularly important to recognise the non-similarity between different 'indigenous peoples' – the only thing that different indigenous peoples have in common is the experience of cultural genocide that has accompanied the last five centuries of Western expansionism.

Questions for discussion or research

- Find out about other cultural traditions concerning the origins of the world, humans and knowledge, and assess how these are similar or dissimilar to the Māori accounts summarised in this chapter.
- Does the translation of philosophical concepts from indigenous languages to English necessarily distort the indigenous concepts, and if so, why? Suggest strategies for working with such distortions.

Suggestions for further reading

Marsden, M., & Henare, T. A. (2003). Kaitiakitanga: a definitive introduction to the holistic world view of the Māori. In T. A. C. Royal (Ed.), *The woven universe* (pp. 54–72).

This book section is a succinct, authoritative account of the traditional Māori view of the world, drawing on the wealth of knowledge of Māori Marsden. This essay was written to assist the development of national legal frameworks for environmental protection, at a time when such ideas seemed more radical and less urgent than they do today. Marsden attempted to contribute the indigenous wisdom of Māori traditions for living in harmony with nature towards a distinctive approach for Aotearoa New Zealand.

Chapter 5: Māori knowledge

Teaching notes

This chapter undertakes two tasks: first, to describe Māori knowledge on its own terms, and second, to describe the difficulties inherent in considering the claims of Māori (or indigenous) knowledge to be something valid but different from Western knowledge. Following an introductory section that explains these inherent contradictions, there is a brief synopsis of the Māori metaphors for knowledge: three baskets and two stones, fetched from the celestial realm for humanity by one of the familial deities already introduced in previous chapters.

The next section is a list of key Māori philosophical concepts, ordered according to the logic of the Māori world view, which showcases the role of each concept within that world view, and how the concepts relate to each other. Following that is another list of traditional Māori words for and about knowledge: words for knowledge, place of learning, expert, think and thought, learn and teach, explain and remember, concept and philosophy. The final section of this chapter returns to consider the defining conundrum at the heart of this book, which can be expressed as a binary: either a claim to delineate Māori philosophy, or a claim that Māori philosophy is impossible to express in a Western language such as English.

Questions for discussion or research

- Discuss the assertion that the Western academic disciplinary structure reflects a Eurocentric world view. If so, what would be the implications? Can you find examples or evidence to either support or contradict this idea – or both?

- Some Māori knowledge concepts bear some resemblance to certain ideas associated with recent radical movements in Western societies such as New Age, Ecosophy or alternative medicine. Find some examples of such concepts, and discuss why such resemblances might exist. Are such conjunctions likely to be favourably viewed by Māori (or other Indigenous) people? Why, or why not?

- Can you find examples of when indigenous knowledge could be argued to give a superior account to that of science?

Suggestions for further reading

Salmond, A. (1978). Te ao tawhito: a semantic approach to the traditional Māori cosmos. *Journal of the Polynesian Society,* *87*(1), 5–28.

Leading New Zealand anthropologist Anne Salmond has studied Māori knowledge for many decades and is currently one of the foremost academic authorities in the field. This journal article sets out the results of Salmond's investigations using semantic approaches based on evidence from within the Māori language itself, and remains one of the best analyses of Māori knowledge I have ever read. It is a difficult but rewarding piece of scholarship with which to engage for the student of Māori philosophy.

Chapter 6: Writing with Māori philosophy

Teaching notes

The first two sections of this chapter summarise my non-empirical research into two topics in Māori education: first, the use of pōwhiri in contemporary education contexts, and second, the story of the famous school journal *Washday at the Pā*. The final section presents three original stories or vignettes in which I have tried to use the power of narrative in academic writing to portray instances of the 'gap' or incommensurability between Māori and Pākehā philosophies and worldviews. The chapter includes more detailed explanatory notes on each of these pieces of writing.

Questions for discussion or research

• Research the use of narrative genres (short stories, poems, etc.) in philosophical scholarship.
• Use creative writing to make a scholarly response to a research topic of personal significance.

Suggestions for further reading

King, T. (2003). *The truth about stories: a native narrative*. Minneapolis: University of Minnesota Press.

Mazer, S., & Papesch, T. R. (2010). Māori performance/cultural performance: stages of powhiri. In Ngā Kete a Rēhua (Ed.), *Inaugural Māori research symposium Te Waipounamu proceedings book* (pp. 276–81). Christchurch, New Zealand: University of Canterbury.

Stewart, G. (2019). Mana Wahine and *Washday at the Pā*. *Educational Philosophy and Theory, 51*(7), 684–92. https://doi.org/10.1080/00131857.2017.1339339

Stewart, G., & Dale, H. (2016). 'Dirty laundry' in Māori education history? Another spin for *Washday at the Pā*. *Waikato Journal of Education, 21*(2), 5–15. https://doi.org/10.15663/wje.v21i2.268

Stewart, G., & Dale, H. (2018). Reading the 'ghost book': Māori talk about *Washday at the Pā*, by Ans Westra. *Video Journal of Education and Pedagogy, 3*(2). Stewart2018. https://doi.org/10.1186/s40990-018-0014-2

Stewart, G., Tamatea, K., & Mika, C. (2015). Infinitely welcome: Education pōwhiri and ethnic performativity. *MAI Journal, 4*(2), 91–103.

References

Ahmed, S. (2000). *Strange encounters: Embodied others in post-coloniality.* London & New York: Routledge.

Alpers, A. (1996). *Māori myths & tribal legends.* Auckland: Longman.

Auckland Art Gallery Toi o Tamaki. (2018). Lindauer Online. Retrieved from http://www.lindaueronline.co.nz/maori-portraits

Barlow, C. (1991). *Tikanga whakaaro: Key concepts in Māori culture.* Oxford, UK: Oxford University Press.

Barton, B. (1993). Ethnomathematics & its place in the classroom. In E. McKinley & P. Waiti (Eds.), *SAMEpapers 1993* (Vol. 1993, pp. 46–68). Hamilton: CSMER Publications.

Battye, S., & Waitai, K. (2011). *He kete o te reo pōwhiri - Pōwhiri in action.* Christchurch: User Friendly Resources.

Bell, A. (2014). *Relating indigenous & settler identities: Beyond domination.* New York, NY: Palgrave Macmillan.

Besley, T., & Peters, M. (Eds.). (2012). *Interculturalism, education & dialogue.* New York: Peter Lang.

Best, E. (2005). *Forest Lore of the Māori.* Wellington: Te Papa Press.

Bhabha, H. (2009). In the cave of making: Thoughts on third space. In K. Ikas & G. Wagner (Eds.), *Communicating in the third space* (pp. ix–xiv). New York: Routledge.

Blommaert, J. (Ed.). (1999). *Language ideological debates.* Berlin & New York: Mouton De Gruyer.

Brookes, B. (2000). Nostalgia for 'innocent homely pleasures': The 1964 New Zealand controversy over Washday at the Pā. In B. Brookes (Ed.), *At home in New Zealand: Houses, history, people* (pp. 210–25). Wellington, New Zealand: Bridget Williams Books.

Bruner, J. (1986). *Actual minds, possible worlds.* Cambridge MA: Harvard University Press.

Butler, J. (2010). Performative agency. *Journal of Cultural Economy, 3*(2), 147–61. doi:10.1080/17530350.2010.494117

Cajete, G. (2000). *Native science: Natural laws of interdependence.* Santa Fe, NM: Clear Light Publishers.

Carpenter, V., & Osborne, S. (2014). *Twelve thousand hours: Education & poverty in Aotearoa New Zealand.* Auckland, New Zealand: Dunmore Press.

Chapman-Taylor, R. (1948). *Life in the Pa*. Wellington: School Publications Branch.

Chase, S. E. (2013). Narrative inquiry - still a field in the making. In N. K. Denzin & Y. S. Lincoln (Eds.), *Collecting & interpreting qualitative materials* (4th ed., pp. 55–83). Thousand Oaks, CA: Sage.

Cobern, W. W. (1991). *World view theory & science education research*. Retrieved from http://scholarworks.wmich.edu/cgi/viewcontent.cgi?artic le=1043&context=science_slcsp

Cooper, R. L., & Spolsky, B. (Eds.). (1991). *The influence of language on culture and thought*. Berlin: Mouton de Gruyter & Co.

Crystal, D. (2000). *Language death*. Cambridge: Cambridge University Press.

Dickison, M. (1994). Māori science? Can traditional Māori knowledge be considered scientific? *New Zealand Science Monthly, 5*(4), 6–7.

Drichel, S. (2008). The time of hybridity. *Philosophy & Social Criticism, 34*(6), 587–615.

Durie, M. H. (2005). *Ngā tai matatū: Tides of Māori endurance*. Melbourne: Oxford University Press.

Dutta, N. (2004). The face of the other. *Interventions: International Journal of Postcolonial Studies, 6*(3), 431–50. doi:10.1080/1369801042000280069

Edwards, H., & Ellmers, K. (2010). *Powhiri: Welcome - or not?* (Documentary). Auckland: Tumanako Productions.

Eriksen, T. H. (2002). *Ethnicity & nationalism* (2nd ed.). London: Pluto Press.

Fine, M. (1994). Working the hyphens: Reinventing self & other in qualitative research. In N. K. Denzin & Y. S. Lincoln (Eds.), *Handbook of qualitative research* (pp. 70–82). Thousand Oaks, CA: Sage.

Firth, R. (1972). *Economics of the New Zealand Māori* (2nd ed.). Wellington: Government Printer.

Fishman, J. A. (1960). A sytematization of the Whorfian hypothesis. *Behavioural Science, 5*, 323–39.

Fishman, J. A. (1980). The Whorfian hypothesis: Varieties of valuation, confirmation and disconfirmation: I. *International Journal of the Sociology of Language, 26*, 25–40.

Fishman, J. A. (1982). Whorfianism of the third kind: Ethnolinguistic diversity as a worldwide societal asset. *Language in Society, 11*, 1–14.

Gottlieb, R. S. (Ed.). (1993). *Radical philosophy: Tradition, counter-tradition, politics*. Philadelphia, PA: Temple University Press.

Gould, S. J. (1997). *The mismeasure of man* (Revised & expanded ed.). London: Penguin.

Grace, P. (1986). Parade. In *Waiariki and other stories* (pp. 81–9). Auckland, NZ: Penguin Books.

Graeber, D. (2012). Dead zones of the imagination: On violence, bureaucracy, & interpretive labour. *Hau: Journal of Ethnographic Theory, 2*(2), 105–28. https://doi.org/http://dx.doi.org/10.14318/hau2.2.007

Halliday, M. A. K. (2004). *The language of science.* London & New York: Continuum.

Hamilton, S. (2017). The white tangata whenua, & other bullshit from the 'One New Zealand' crew. Retrieved from https://thespinoff.co.nz/socie ty/22-05-2017/the-white-tangata-whenua-&-other-bullshit-from-the-one-new-zealand-crew/

Hanson, A. (1989). The making of the Maori: Culture invention and its logic. *American Anthropologist, 91*(4), 890–902.

Hanson, F. A., & Hanson, L. (1983). *Counterpoint in Māori culture.* London: Routledge & Kegan Paul.

Hastrup, K. (1982). Establishing an ethnicity: The emergence of the 'Icelanders' in the early middle ages. In D. Parkin (Ed.), *Semantic anthropology* (pp. 145–60). London & New York: Academic Press.

Heidegger, M. (1977). *The question concerning technology & other essays.* New York: Harper Torchbooks.

Herman, D. (Ed.). (2003). *Narrative theory & the cognitive sciences.* Stanford: CSLI Publications.

Herrnstein, R. J., & Murray, C. A. (1996). *The bell curve: Intelligence & class structure in American life* (1st Free Press pbk. ed.. ed.). New York: Simon & Schuster.

Herrnstein Smith, B. (2005). *Scandalous knowledge: Science, truth & the human.* Edinburgh: Edinburgh University Press Ltd.

Hoskins, T. K. (2012). A fine risk: Ethics in Kaupapa Māori politics. *New Zealand Journal of Education Studies. Te Hautaka Mātai Mātauranga, 47*(2), 85–99.

Hoyningen-Huene, P., & Sankey, H. (Eds.). (2001). *Incommensurability & related matters.* Dordrecht, Boston and London: Kluwer Academic Publishers.

Ihimaera, W. (1985). Ans Westra: Holder of the mirror (introduction). In A. Westra & K. Mataira (Eds.), *Whaiora: The pursuit of life.* Wellington: Unwin.

Jackson, M. (1992). The Treaty & the word: The colonization of Māori philosophy. In G. Oddie & R. Perrett (Eds.), *Justice, ethics & New Zealand society* (pp. 1–10). Oxford, UK: Oxford University Press.

Jones, A. (1999). The limits of cross-cultural dialogue: Pedagogy, desire and absolution in the classroom. *Educational Theory, 49*(3), 299–316.

Jones, A. (2001). Cross-cultural pedagogy & the passion for ignorance. *Feminism & Psychology, 11*(3), 279–92. DOI: 10.1177/0959353501011003002

Jones, A. (2005). Pedagogy of the gaps: Lessons on evidence, from the beach. In B. Webber (Ed.), *The Herbison lectures, 1999–2004* (pp. 7–33). Wellington: NZCER Press.

Jones, A., & Jenkins, K. (2008). Rethinking collaboration: Working the indigene-colonizer hyphen. In N. K. Denzin, Y. S. Lincoln, & L. T. Smith (Eds.), *Handbook of critical & indigenous methodologies* (pp. 471–86). Los Angeles, CA: Sage.

Keown, M. (2013). 'Sheddings of light': Patricia Grace & Māori short fiction. In M. Awadalla & P. March-Russell (Eds.), *The postcolonial short story* (pp. 33–48). Houndmills, UK: Palgrave Macmillan.

King, T. (2003). *The truth about stories: A native narrative.* Minneapolis: University of Minnesota Press.

Lamb, S. (2004). Philosophical differences & cognitive styles. In S. Lamb (Ed.), *Language & reality* (pp. 496–502). London & New York: Continuum.

Lee, P. (1996). *The Whorf theory complex: A critical reconstruction.* Amsterdam/Philadelphia: John Benjamins Publishing Company.

Locke, T. (2004). *Critical discourse analysis.* London & New York: Continuum.

Lomax, T. (1996). Māori science revisited. *NZ Science Monthly, 7*(6), 12–13.

Lyotard, J.-F. (1988). *The differend: Phrases in dispute* (G. V. D. Abbeele, Trans.): Manchester University Press.

Matenga-Kohu, J., & Roberts, J. (2006). *Pōwhiri: Rituals of encounter.* Cambridge: Wotz Wot Ltd.

Mauss, M. (1990). *The gift: The form & reason for exchange in archaic societies* (W. D. Halls, Trans.). New York: Norton.

May, S. (2012). *Language & minority rights: Ethnicity, nationalism & the politics of language* (2nd ed.). New York: Routledge.

Mazer, S., & Papesch, T. R. (2010). Māori performance/cultural performance: Stages of powhiri. In Ngā Kete a Rēhua (Ed.), *Inaugural Māori research symposium Te Waipounamu proceedings book* (pp. 276–81). Christchurch, New Zealand: University of Canterbury.

McDonald, L. (1988). Ragged house photographs: Ans Westra's *Washday at the Pā. Photofile, 6*(3), 18–23.

McDonald, L. (2012). *Camera Antipode Ans Westra: Photography as a form of ethnographic & historical writing*. (PhD), Massey University.

McHoul, A. W., & Grace, W. (1998). *A foucault primer: Discourse, power, & the subject*. Dunedin, NZ: University of Otago Press.

McKinley, E. (2003). *Brown bodies, white coats: Postcolonialism, Māori women & science*. (Unpublished Doctor of Philosophy thesis), University of Waikato, Hamilton, New Zealand.

Menzies, T. T. A. (1993). From *E pā tō hau*. In W. Ihimaera (Ed.), *Te Ao Mārama 2* (pp. 54–7). Auckland: Reed.

Menzies, T. T. A., & Maihi, T. T. R. (1986). *Uenuku*. Auckland: Waiata Koa.

Metge, J. (2010). *Tuamaka: The challenge of difference in Aotearoa New Zealand*. Auckland: Auckland University Press.

Metge, J. (2015). *Tauira: Māori methods of learning and teaching*. Auckland: Auckland University Press.

Mika, C. (2012). Overcoming 'being' in favour of knowledge: The fixing effect of 'mātauranga'. *Educational Philosophy & Theory, 44*(10), 1080–92. doi:10.1111/j.1469-5812.2011.00771.x

Mika, C. (2015). The thing's revelation: Some thoughts on Māori philosophical research. *Waikato Journal of Education, 20*(2), 61–8. https://wje.org.nz/index.php/WJE/article/view/206

Mika, C. (2017). *Indigenous education & the metaphysics of presence: A worlded philosophy*. Oxon, UK: Routledge.

Mikaere, B. (2013). *Māori in Aotearoa New Zealand: Understanding the culture, protocols & customs*. Auckland: New Holland.

Ministry of Education. (2008). *Te Marautanga o Aotearoa*. Wellington: Learning Media.

Moewaka-Barnes, A., Borell, B., Taiapa, K., Rankine, J., & McCreanor, T. (2012). Anti-Māori themes in New Zealand journalism - toward alternative practice. *Pacific Journalism Review, 18*(1), 195–216.

Moorehead, A. (1968). *The fatal impact*. Harmondsworth, UK: Penguin.

New Zealand Treasury. (1987). *Government management: Brief to the incoming government, Vol 2, education issues*. Wellington, NZ: New Zealand Government.

Openshaw, R. (2001). Diverting the flak: The response of the New Zealand Department of Education to curriculum controversy. *Change: Transformations in Education, 4*(1), 33–47.

Openshaw, R. (2005). '... Nothing objectionable or controversial': The image of Māori ethnicity & 'difference' in New Zealand social studies. In Y. Nozaki, R. Openshaw, & A. Luke (Eds.), *Struggles over difference: Curriculum, texts, & pedagogy in the Asia-Pacific* (pp. 25–40). Albany NY: State of New York University Press.

Otago Daily Times. (1964, 23 July). Māori women incensed by bulletin issued by Education Department. *Otago Daily Times.*

Patterson, J. (1992). *Exploring Māori values.* Palmerston North: Dunmore Press.

Patterson, J. (2000). *People of the land: A Pacific philosophy.* Palmerston North, NZ: Dunmore Press.

Penetito, W. (2010). *What's Māori about Māori education?* Wellington, New Zealand: Victoria University Press.

Peters, M. (1993). *Post-modern science in Aotearoa? conservation, cosmology & critique.* Auckland, New Zealand: Research Unit for Māori Education, University of Auckland.

Pihama, L. (2001). *Tihei mauri ora - honouring our voices: Mana wahine as a kaupapa Māori theoretical framework* (Unpublished PhD), University of Auckland.

Pihama, L. (2012). A short commentary on *Boy. New Zealand Journal of Media Studies, 13*(1), 97–103. Retrieved from http://ndhadeliver.natlib.govt.nz/delivery/DeliveryManagerServlet?dps_pid=FL13954894

Pihama, L., Cram, F., & Walker, S. (2002). Creating methodological space: A literature review of Kaupapa Maori research. *Canadian Journal of Native Education, 26*(1), 30–43.

Pihama, L., Smith, K., Taki, M., & Lee, J. B. J. (2004). *A literature review on Kaupapa Māori & Māori education pedagogy.* Auckland, NZ: IRI - International Research Institute for Māori & Indigenous Education.

Radio New Zealand. (2013). Cartoon 'appalling, but not racism'. Retrieved from https://www.radionz.co.nz/news/national/136461/cartoon-%27appalling,-but-not-racism%27

Rangihau, J. (1992). Being Māori. In M. King (Ed.), *Te ao hurihuri* (pp. 183–90). Auckland: Reed.

Rata, E. (2012). Theoretical claims & empirical evidence in Māori education discourse. *Educational Philosophy & Theory, 44*(10), 1060–72. doi:10.1111/j.1469-5812.2011.00755.x

Rau-Kapa, M. (1993). The Mobil connection. In W. Ihimaera (Ed.), *Te Ao Mārama 2* (pp. 210–12). Auckland: Reed.

Reedy, T. (1992). *Kura Kaupapa Māori: he mahinga rangahau me te whakapakari: Te pūrongo whakamutunga/Kura Kaupapa Māori, research & development project final report.* Wellington: Ministry of Education.

Roberts, M. (1998). Indigenous knowledge & western science: Perspectives from the Pacific. In D. Hodson (Ed.), *Science & technology education & ethnicity: An Aotearoa New Zealand perspective* (pp. 59–75). Wellington, NZ: The Royal Society of New Zealand.

Roberts, M., Haami, B. J. T. M., Benton, R., Satterfield, T., Finucane, M. L., Henare, M., & Henare, M. (2004). Whakapapa as a Māori mental construct: Some implications for the debate over genetic modification of organisms. *The Contemporary Pacific, 16*(1), 1–28.

Roberts, P. (2013). Academic dystopia: Knowledge, performativity & tertiary education. *The Review of Education, Pedagogy, & Cultural Studies, 35*(1), 27–43. https://doi.org/10.1080/10714413.2013.753757

Roberts, P., & Peters, M. (2008). *Neoliberalism, higher education & research.* Rotterdam: Sense Publishers.

Robin, R. (1991). They separate the mana. *Te Whakamārama: Māori law bulletin,* (10), 3–4.

Royal, T. A. C. (Ed.). (2003). *The Woven Universe: Selected writings of Rev. Māori Marsden:* The Estate of Rev. Māori Marsden.

Salmond, A. (1978). Te ao tawhito: A semantic approach to the traditional Māori cosmos. *Journal of the Polynesian Society, 87*(1), 5–28.

Salmond, A. (1985). Māori epistemologies. In J. Overing (Ed.), *Reason & morality* (pp. 237–60). London & New York: Tavistock Publications.

Salmond, A. (1997). *Between worlds.* Auckland: Viking - Penguin Books (NZ) Ltd.

Salmond, A. (2012). Ontological quarrels: Indigeneity, exclusion & citizenship in a relational world. *Anthropological Theory, 12*(2), 115–41.

Sapir, E. (1933). Language. In *Encyclopedia of the social sciences* (Vol. 9, pp. 155–69). New York: Macmillan.

Schlesinger, I. M. (1991). The wax & wane of Whorfian views. In R. L. Cooper & B. Spolsky (Eds.), *The influence of language on culture & thought.* Berlin: Mouton de Gruyter.

Sharples, P. (1994). Kura Kaupapa Māori. In H. McQueen (Ed.), *Education is change* (pp. 11–21). Wellington, NZ: Bridget Williams Books.

Siegel, H. (2006). Epistemological diversity & education research: Much ado about nothing much? *Educational Researcher, 35*(2), 3–12.

Simmonds, N. (2011). Mana Wahine: Decolonising politics. *Womens Studies Journal, 25*(2), 11–25.

Smallman, E. R. (2016). *Government announces land wars day at Tūrangawaewae.* Retrieved from http://www.stuff.co.nz/national/83329239 /Government-announces-Land-Wars-Day-at-Turangawaewae

Smith, C. W.-I.-T.-R. (2000). Straying beyond the boundaries of belief: Māori epistemologies inside the curriculum. *Educational Philosophy & Theory, 32*(1), 43–51.

Smith, G. H. (1986). Taha Māori: A Pākehā privilege. *Delta, 37,* 11–23.

Smith, G. H. (1997). *The development of Kaupapa Māori: Theory & praxis.* (PhD), University of Auckland, Auckland, New Zealand.

Smith, G. H. (2003). *Kaupapa Māori theory: Theorizing indigenous transformation of education & schooling.* Paper presented at the AARE/ NZARE, Auckland, New Zealand. http://www.aare.edu.au/data/publica tions/2003/pih03342.pdf

Smith, G. H. (2012). Interview: Kaupapa Māori: The dangers of domestication. *New Zealand Journal of Educational Studies, 47*(2), 10–20.

Smith, L. T. (2012). *Decolonizing methodologies: Research & indigenous peoples* (2nd ed.). London/New York & Dunedin: Zed Books & Otago University Press.

Smith, T. (2000). Ngā Tini Āhuatanga o Whakapapa Kōrero. *Educational Philosophy & Theory, 32*(1), 53–60.

Sokal, A. D. (1996a). Transgressing the boundaries: An afterword. *Philosophy & Literature, 20,* 338–46.

Sokal, A. D. (1996b). Transgressing the boundaries: Toward a transformative hermeneutics of quantum gravity. *Social Text, 14*(46/47 Special Issue on 'Science Wars'), 217–52.

Stenhouse, J. (1999). Darwinism in New Zealand. In R. L. Numbers & J. Stenhouse (Eds.), *Disseminating darwinism* (pp. 61–89). Cambridge: Cambridge University Press.

Stewart, G. (2007). *Kaupapa Māori science* (EdD), Unpublished doctoral thesis in Education, Waikato University, Hamilton.

Stewart, G. (2017a). The 'hau' of research: Mauss meets Kaupapa Māori. *Journal of World Philosophies, 2*(1), 1–11. doi:10.2979/jourworlphil.2.1.01

Stewart, G. (2017b). Kaupapa Māori theory as a philosophy for education. In T. K. Hoskins & A. Jones (Eds.), *Critical conversations in Kaupapa Māori* (pp. 133–46). Wellington: Huia Publishers.

Stewart, G., & Dale, H. (2016). 'Dirty laundry' in Māori education history? Another spin for Washday at the Pā. *Waikato J Educ, 21.* doi:10.15663/wje.v21i2.268

Stewart, G., Tamatea, K., & Mika, C. (2015). Infinitely welcome: Education pōwhiri & ethnic performativity. *MAI J, 4,* 91–103.

Stewart, G., Trinick, T., & Dale, H. (2017). Te Marautanga o Aotearoa: History of a national Māori curriculum. *Curriculum Matters, 13,* 8–20. doi:https://doi.org/10.18296/cm.0018

Stokes, J. (2006, 30 September 2006). Full-blooded challenge to Don Brash. *NZ Herald.* Retrieved from http://www.nzherald.co.nz/nz/news/article.cfm?c_id=1&objectid=10403690

Stuff. (2013). 'Racist' cartoon slammed. Retrieved from http://www.stuff.co.nz/national/8736295/Racist-cartoon-slammed

Tawake, S. (2000). Transforming the insider-outsider perspective: Postcolonial fiction from the Pacific. *The Contemporary Pacific, 12*(1), 155–75.

Te Ara - The Encyclopedia of New Zealand. (2018a). The dying Māori & Social Darwinism. Retrieved from https://teara.govt.nz/en/european-ideas-about-maori/page-4

Te Ara - The Encyclopedia of New Zealand. (2018b). New Zealand Wars. Retrieved from https://teara.govt.nz/en/new-zealand-wars

Te Papa Tongarewa. (1998). Washday at the Pā controversy. Retrieved from http://collections.tepapa.govt.nz/topic/952

The Spinoff. (2018). Bob Jones & NBR divorce over 'Māori Gratitude Day' column. Retrieved from https://thespinoff.co.nz/media/07-02-2018/bob-jones-&-nbr-divorce-over-maori-appreciation-day-column/

Walker, R. J. (1989). Māori identity. In D. Novitz & B. Willmott (Eds.), *Culture & identity in New Zealand* (pp. 35–52). Wellington: GP Books.

Walker, S., Eketone, A., & Gibbs, A. (2006). An exploration of kaupapa Māori research, its principles, processes & applications. *International Journal of Social Research Methodology, 9*(4), 331–44.

Webster, S. (1998). *Patrons of Maori culture: Power, theory & ideology in the Maori renaissance.* Dunedin: University of Otago Press.

Westra, A. (1964). *Washday at the Pā* (Rev. ed.). Christchurch, NZ: Caxton Press.

Westra, A., & Amery, M. (2011). *Washday at the Pā*. Wellington: Suite Publishing.

Wetherell, M., & Potter, J. (1992). *Mapping the language of racism: Discourse & the legitimation of exploitation*. New York: Harvester Wheatsheaf.

Whorf, B. L. (1956). *Language, thought & reality*. Cambridge, MA: The M.I.T. Press.

Wikipedia. (2018). Ngā Tamatoa. Retrieved from https://en.wikipedia.org/wiki/Ng%C4%81_Tamatoa

Williams, H. W. (1971). *A Dictionary of the Māori language* (7th ed.). Wellington: GP Publications.

Willmott, B. (1989). Introduction: Culture & national identity. In D. Novitz & B. Willmott (Eds.), *Culture & identity in New Zealand* (pp. 1–20). Wellington: GP Books.

Wilson, B. R. (Ed.). (1970). *Rationality*. Oxford: Basil Blackwell.

Wright, M. (2017). *Tribunal finds 'provocative' Fairfax cartoons did not breach Human Rights Act*. Retrieved from https://www.stuff.co.nz/national/92502908/tribunal-finds-provocative-fairfax-cartoons-did-not-breach-human-rights-act

Index